The Masters of Eventing

The Masters of Eventing

Edited by G. W. Freeman
Photography by G. A. Marston

Lucinda Prior-Palmer

Karl Schultz

Aly Adsetts

Bruce Davidson

Chris Collins

Richard Meade

Jane Holderness-Roddam

Lady Hugh Russell

Diana Thorne

Jane Starkey

Rachel Bayliss

Lt. Col. Bill Lithgow

Horst Karsten

Mike Plumb

Sarah Glyn

Celia Ross-Taylor

EYRE METHUEN . LONDON

Contents

Preface

In every sporting activity, there are those that are the best. The rest perhaps wonder why they are not so good and seek to find the magical combination of strength, timing, planning, equipment and training that will produce better results. This book is about the best in eventing – one of the sports that involves another living being as a partner – and in particular about those riders who in international competition have emerged as the current "Masters".

The process of selecting the Masters was hard, especially when it came to looking for expertise on a specific subject, and our selection committee settled for a degree of arbitrariness that may cause debate. Dividing the book into subjects and allocating a subject to the most appropriate Master, we embarked on a detailed and intensive interview with each Master which was later reduced into a readable form.

We were expecting to find a similarity of technique – a sort of "approved method" – but this didn't quite happen. The different mental approach and physical make-up of each Master has a vital effect on technique, producing interesting variations and in a few cases an opposite view to the accepted text-book procedure.

Although all the Masters involved demonstrated a professional approach to the business of competing successfully at international level, every one of them emerged as being truly amateur in terms of affection and personal enthusiasm for their chosen sport.

Acknowledgements

I give my personal thanks to:

All the Masters for the courteous way in which they made available valuable time for the interviews.

Joanna Boswell and her colleagues in the Combined Training Office at Stoneleigh who provided vital research information.

The Editorial Team who, although they hadn't worked together before, made it a pleasure to be involved in this project.

Ann Mansbridge at Eyre Methuen who thought this book was a good idea in the first place.

Jane Pontifex who cheered us on and also created the concluding chapter.

Leslie Lane who took the photographs used in Chapter 17.

Frank Sanford in Omaha, genius of the brief informative telex.

My wife, whose advice helped me greatly and to whom, with affection, I dedicate this book.

Geoffrey Freeman 1978

First published 1978
© 1978 G.W. Freeman
Printed in Great Britain for
Eyre Methuen Ltd
11 New Fetter Lane, London EC4P 4EE
By Hazell, Watson & Viney Ltd
Aylesbury, Bucks

ISBN 0 413 38580 9

Editorial Team

Editor and Interviewer

Geoffrey Freeman is the Chairman of a major international advertising agency and became involved in Horse Trials in 1970. His fascination with the skills and talent of the great competitors of today at the highest levels of eventing is the main reason for the existence of this book.

Photography

Geoffrey Marston is a well-known professional photographer specialising in equestrian subjects. He has been in the horse world all his life, joined the Royal Army Veterinary Corps (he won the Prince of Wales Cup for show jumping during his service) and became an instructor at the Army School of Equitation. When he left the army to establish his photographic career he became particularly well-known for his intelligent covering of the eventing scene.

Art Director

Don Wellman is the Creative Director of the same company as the Editor. During an outstanding career in the world of commercial art he has gained a considerable reputation as an innovator, illustrator and designer.

Technical Editor

Major R.M. Burke has enjoyed a brilliant army and equestrian career. He instructed at the famous Weedon army school of equitation, was a member of the British Show Jumping Team and was Chief Instructor at Porlock. 'Paddy' Burke recently successfully competed in the Veterans Section at the Crookham Horse Trials.

Editorial Co-ordinator

Nick Thornley worked for the BBC for seven years including two years with Huw Wheldon when he was Head of Documentary Films. In 1972 he devised a documentary film on the Munich Olympic Games called "Champions" which went out on BBC Grandstand and ABC New York. Now Managing Director of a Company in London, Nick also does freelance broadcasting for BBC Radio.

Foreword

Reading this book I might be sitting at the fireside talking to friends in the event world, their voices come out through the written word, and even without knowing who had written each chapter, I can hear them talking and know each one. From the very successful young lady who trained in the discotheque at Annabels to the current World Champion, their words and their voices are unmistakable.

For those who think themselves to be experts in eventing to the beginner who is starting to take up this sport, there is much to be learnt and much to discuss.

This is not a training text book but thoughts of individuals who have learnt their sport from hard experience and there is a wealth of sound, practical, commonsense ways and means of making eventing easier for both rider and horse, of things to ignore and things to remember. I wish this book had been written twenty-five years ago when I was competing. We had to learn from our own mistakes, by trial and error; this book gives the beginner an insight into the sport through the eyes and experience of others and will give them a lot to think about and remember.

My only regret is that it is not entitled 'The Eventer's Bedside Book', because that is where it belongs for reading last thing at night either when problems have arisen in training a horse during the day or making a check list for the event tomorrow.

Major A.L. Rook, M.C.
Chairman of the Combined Training Group

The Masters

Lady Hugh Russell

Prior to her accident, Lady Hugh Russell used to ride in one-two- and three-day events, always riding horses she had broken and produced herself. When she broke her back in a hunting accident in 1976, Lady Hugh lent her horse, Turnstone, on whom she had many successes in national and international events, to Richard Meade. For the last sixteen years Lady Hugh has organised the Wylye Horse Trials, now a full-scale international three-day event, and not only designs the Wylye cross-country course, but is frequently asked to advise other organisers on course design.

Since she has been unable to ride, Lady Hugh has concentrated on helping riders with producing event horses and particularly with cross-country jumping training. Her mini-moke enables her to walk the courses at events with competitors to help them plan their cross-country rides. Lady Hugh travels to almost all the major three-day events at home and abroad. The mini-moke which she uses as her legs has become a familiar sight to event riders all over the world.

Aly Adsetts

Has been competing in Horse Trials since 1969.
1974 4th Midland Bank Novice Championships (Bleak Hills)
1st Midland Bank Open Championships (Carawich)
1st Tidworth Three-Day Event (Olivia)
1975 1st Burghley C.C.I. (Carawich)
1977 5th Badminton C.C.I. (Carawich)
6th Midland Bank Open Championships (Carawich)
10th Burghley C.C.I.O.– European Championships –(Carawich) Nominated Individual

Diana Thorne

Has been competing in Horse Trials since 1971.
1972 1st Midland Bank Novice Championships (The Kingmaker)
1973 5th Tidworth Three-Day Event (The Kingmaker)
2nd Burghley C.C.I. (The Kingmaker)
1974 3rd Tidworth Three-Day Event (The Kingmaker)
1975 1st Haras du Pin C.C.I. (The Kingmaker)
10th Burghley C.C.I. (The Kingmaker)
5th Midland Bank Open Championships (The Kingmaker)
1977 2nd Badminton C.C.I. (The Kingmaker)
4th Burghley C.C.I.O. European Championships (The Kingmaker)
Diana was the first lady rider to win a steeplechase under National Hunt Rules.

Rachel Bayliss

Has been competing in Horse Trials since 1970.
1971 5th Tidworth Three-Day Event (Gurgle The Greek)
1973 Gurgle The Greek made history by being the only horse to pass unscathed under the Stockholm fence at Badminton C.C.I.
1974 2nd Tidworth Three-Day Event (Gurgle The Greek)
2nd Midland Bank Open Championships (Gurgle The Greek)
1975 2nd Midland Bank Open Championships (Gurgle The Greek)
1976 1st Midland Bank Open Championships (Gurgle The Greek)
1977 1st Midland Bank Novice Championships (Mystic Minstrel)
Gurgle The Greek has won more One-Day Horse Trials than any other horse to date.

Jane Starkey

Has been competing in Horse Trials since 1972.
1973 6th Burghley C.C.I. (Acrobat)
6th Boekelo C.C.I. (Acrobat)
1974 3rd Bramham Three-Day Event (Acrobat)
2nd Antwerp C.C.I. (Topper Too)
1975 1st Antwerp C.C.I. (Acrobat)
4th Haras du Pin C.C.I. (Topper Too)
6th Burghley C.C.I. (Acrobat)
1976 8th Badminton C.C.I. (Topper Too)
4th Burghley C.C.I. (Topper Too)
3rd Midland Bank Open Championships (Topper Too)
1977 7th Antwerp C.C.I. (Topper Too)
4th Midland Bank Open Championships (Topper Too)
12th Burghley C.C.I.O. European Championships (Topper Too)
(Topper Too was reserve horse at Montreal and winner of the
Calcutta Light Horse Trophy)

Jane Holderness-Roddam

Has been competing since 1965. Jane was the first woman to ride
in an Olympic Three-Day Event.
1967 5th Badminton C.C.I. (Our Nobby)
3rd Burghley C.C.I. (Our Nobby)
1968 1st Badminton C.C.I. (Our Nobby)
3rd Burghley C.C.I. (Our Nobby)
Member of Gold Medal winning Team at Olympic Games,
Mexico (Our Nobby)
1976 1st Burghley C.C.I. (Warrior)
1977 4th Badminton C.C.I. (Warrior)
2nd Tidworth Three-Day Event (Just So)
7th Midland Bank Open Championships (Just So)
5th Burghley C.C.I.O. European Championships and also a
member of the winning team (Warrior).

Horst Karsten

1963 3rd Munich C.C.I. (Hanko)
1964 6th individually and a member of the Bronze Medal winning
Team at Olympic Games, Tokyo (Condora)
1965 3rd Moscow C.C.I.O. European Championships (Condora)
1972 6th Burghley C.C.I. (Sioux)
Member of Bronze Medal winning Team at Olympic Games,
Munich (Sioux)
1973 3rd Kiev C.C.I.O. European Championships and member
of winning Team (Sioux)
1976 Member of Silver Medal winning Team at Olympic Games,
Montreal
3rd Luhmühlen C.C.I. (Sioux)
1st Boekelo C.C.I. (Sioux)
1977 1st Luhmühlen C.C.I. (Sioux)
3rd Burghley C.C.I.O. European Championships (Sioux)
1st Boekelo C.C.I. (Sioux)

Lucinda Prior-Palmer

Lucinda has been competing since 1969. The only rider to be
European Champion twice.
1973 1st Badminton C.C.I. (Be Fair)
1st Luhmühlen C.C.I.O. European Championships (Be Fair) and
member of G.B. Team placed 2nd.
1st Boekelo C.C.I. (Wide Awake)
1976 1st Badminton C.C.I. (Wide Awake)
3rd Tidworth Three-Day Event (Village Gossip)
2nd Burghley C.C.I. (Killaire)
1977 1st Badminton C.C.I. (George)
3rd Badminton C.C.I. (Killaire)
2nd Luhmühlen C.C.I. (Village Gossip)
2nd Midland Bank Open Championships (George)
1st Burghley C.C.I.O. European Championships (George) and a
member of the winning team
3rd Ledyard Farm C.C.I. (Killaire)
2nd Boekelo C.C.I. (Village Gossip)

The Masters

Bruce Davidson

1974 3rd Badminton C.C.I. (Irish Cap)
1st Burghley C.C.I.O. World Championships (Irish Cap) and also a member of the winning team
1975 1st Pan American Games (Golden Griffin)
1976 10th Individually Montreal Olympic Games and also a member of the Gold Medal winning team (Irish Cap)
Golden Griffin was produced in Great Britain by Bertie Hill.

Richard Meade O.B.E.

Richard started competing in B.H.S. Horse Trials in 1961. He is the holder of three Olympic Gold Medals, having been a member of the Gold Medal winning team in Mexico 1968 and a member of the victorious British team in Munich 1972, where he also won the Individual Gold Medal. Richard was 4th at the 1976 Olympic Games, Montreal.
1968 4th Olympic Games Mexico (Cornishman V) and also a member of the Gold Medal winning team.
1970 1st Badminton C.C.I. (The Poacher)
1st Olympic Games, Munich and also a member of the Gold Medal winning Team (Laurieston)
1973 2nd Badminton C.C.I. (Eagle Rock)
1st Boekelo C.C.I. (Wayfarer II)
1st Tidworth Three-Day Event (Jacob Jones)
1975 1st Bramham Three-Day Event (Jacob Jones)
1976 4th Badminton C.C.I. (Jacob Jones)
4th Olympic Games, Montreal (Jacob Jones)

Sarah Glynn

Sarah has been competing since 1971.
1974 3rd Tidworth Three-Day Event (The Wheeler Dealer)
1975 7th Punchestown C.C.I. (The Wheeler Dealer)
1976 1st Middleton Park C.C.I. (The Wheeler Dealer)
1st Tidworth Three-Day Event (The Wheeler Dealer)
2nd Boekelo C.C.I. (The Wheeler Dealer)

Mike Plumb

1963 Member of winning team at Pan American Games
1964 Member of Silver Medal winning team at Olympic Games, Tokyo
1967 Member of winning team at Pan American Games
1968 Member of Silver Medal winning team at Olympic Games, Mexico
1971 Classified leading Three-Day Event rider in U.S.A., for fifth time in seven years
1972 Member of Silver Medal winning team at Olympic Games, Munich
1973 2nd Ledyard Farm C.C.I. (West Country)
3rd Ledyard Farm C.C.I. (Jonny O)
1974 Member of winning team at Burghley C.C.I.O. World Championships and 2nd individually (Good Mixture)
1976 Member of Gold Medal winning team at Olympic Games, Montreal and 2nd individually (Better and Better)
1977 1st Ledyard Farm C.C.I. (Laurenson)
2nd Ledyard Farm C.C.I. (Better and Better)

Chris Collins

Chris has twice won the Swedish Grand National and once the famous Pardubice Race in Czechoslovakia. He has also been Champion Amateur National Hunt Jockey. Chris has been competing in Horse Trials since 1969.

1972 Member of the British team at Burghley C.C.I.O. World Championships placed 2nd (Smokey VI)
1973 4th Burghley C.C.I. (Centurion)
3rd Boekelo C.C.I. (Smokey VI)
4th Tidworth Three-Day Event (Barber's Peace)
2nd Boekelo C.C.I. (Centurion)
1975 1st Tidworth Three-Day Event (Thor IV)
6th Boekelo C.C.I. (Radway)
2nd Midland Bank Open Championships (Smokey VI)
3rd Antwerp C.C.I. (Thor IV)
3rd Midland Bank Open Championships (Smokey VI)
7th Burghley C.C.I.O. European Championships and member of the winning team (SmokeyVI)

Karl Schultz

1969 17th Haras du Pin C.C.I.O. European Championships (Adrian)
1972 6th Individually and member of Bronze Medal winning Team Olympic Games Munich (Pisco)
3rd Boekelo C.C.I. (Wikinger)
1973 3rd Antwerp C.C.I. (Bene)
3rd Kiev C.C.I.O. European Championships and member of winning Team (Sioux)
1974 Member of team placed 3rd Burghley C.C.I.O. World Championships
3rd Boekelo C.C.I. (Twelfth Night)
1975 8th Luhmühlen C.C.I.O. European Championships (Madrigal)
1st Achselschwang C.C.I. (The Monk)
1976 3rd Olympic Games, Montreal and member of Silver Medal winning Team (Madrigal)
1977 9th Badminton C.C.I.
2nd Burghley C.C.I.O. European Championships and member of team placed 2nd (Madrigal)

Celia Ross-Taylor

Celia has been competing since 1961.
1966 1st Tidworth Three-Day Event (Jonathan)
1967 1st Badminton C.C.I. (Jonathan)
1969 6th Badminton C.C.I. (Jonathan)
1st Tidworth Three-Day Event (Jonathan)
1973 7th Tidworth Three-Day Event (Master Question)
4th Midland Bank Open Championships (Master Question)
4th Wylye Three-Day Event (Master Question)
1974 5th Tidworth Three-Day Event (Master Question)

Lt. Colonel W.S.P. Lithgow

Managed the British Three-Day Event Team from 1965, when the European Championships were held in Moscow, right up to and including the Olympic Games in Montreal in 1976. The British team won the Gold Medal in the Mexico and Munich Olympic Games in 1968 and 1972. He is now the Chairman of Selectors.

Bill Lithgow was an Instructor at Sandhurst from 1950 to 1954 where he was Master of the Drag Hunt. He has done point-to-pointing, show jumping and eventing, and though he has competed twice at Badminton, he has sadly never completed the course, one year being eliminated at the last fence. He commanded the 10th Hussars in Germany and Aden from 1961 to 1965.

Chapter 1

Walking a Course
Lady Hugh Russell

How important is walking a course?

Walking a course is undoubtedly one of the secrets for a successful cross-country round and much more important now than it was twenty years ago. There are many more multiple obstacles and alternative fences, and the old saying "Gallop on at the middle" can frequently be disastrous. Modern riders have to plan their routes very carefully and remember that accuracy of line and approach can be vital; gone are the days when you arrived on the morning of the competition, walked rapidly round the course once, and set off on your ride, remembering to keep white flags on the left and red on the right.

How many times should you walk the course?

Preferably three and sometimes four times, so a rider has to be fit himself to do all that walking. The first walk round is basically to give the rider an overall impression of the fences and the route between them. However, you must remember during this view-ing that your first impression of the fences will be the way the horse will see them during the actual round, and so these first impressions for the rider are terribly important and cannot be repeated. Once a rider has walked the course, he knows for example that there is a good landing behind a seemingly bottomless drop; that an apparently innocent little hedge conceals a big ditch; or that a confusing conglomeration of post and rails is only a straightforward in and out. The rider must think all the time of what the horse's reaction must be and he must also visualise the fence surrounded by spectators who might be there during the competition.

What sort of things should the rider look for?

He should look at the fence from twenty to thirty yards away, and consider that all-important first impression. He should then walk slowly forwards, taking careful note of how the fence takes shape.

This view of the fence at the first sighting is vitally important and the rider must think of

The choice of route at one jump will be greatly influenced by the problems presented at the next, and later, obstacles.

One jump takes less out of the horse than two, and is almost always quicker.

It is essential that the rider does his final walk absolutely alone so that he can really concentrate.

the horse's reaction and ride accordingly. Some fences appear low and easy from a distance so the horse is likely to seize the bit several strides back, only to drop behind it when unexpected horrors loom into view. Other fences viewed from afar can look enormous when in fact they might be quite simple.

I also always advise a rider to check the number on every fence as it is very easy to miss a jump on some courses. On the first walk round, too, riders should always stop and memorise the fences and the route so far, after every five or six fences.

Other things he should look for are the state of the ground on the take-off and landing areas and whether they are likely to get slippery, or badly "poached" and possibly boggy later in the day.

What about the going between fences? Is that an important factor?

Varying going from rough to level, from hard to soft, has a great effect on the way horses cope with the course and how sound and happy they will be at the finish. Sometimes you can spend too much time and attention studying fences and forget about the going. This was most noticeable in the Montreal Olympics when the terrain between fences had a tremendous influence because it changed endlessly with the many ditches and hazards, and was very upsetting

to the horse's stride and rhythm. There were some very tired horses on the final day.

All woodland tracks demand special attention for roots, hidden tree stumps and low overhanging branches. A rider on a seventeen-hand horse has to remember to look upwards as well as down.

How about alternative fences?

All the possibilities must be carefully noted and you must pay particular attention to flagging and numbering as well as penalty zones. But it is foolish to make definite decisions about these in the first walk round. I think the first walk round should involve concentration on trying to remember the individual fences and the rider can then think through the fences in sequence and decide on his plan of attack.

You should also look backwards fairly frequently when walking the course to ensure that you are taking the best line between fences. Organisers have a nasty habit of positioning markers off route, because they find a tree to hang them on which is easier than putting in another stake.

Do you recommend short cuts?

Some riders, and Sheila Willcox was an expert, are specialists in finding short cuts that can save valuable seconds, but beware! Turning flags can easily be missed and for this you can be eliminated, so check it out

Jumping the fences clear is obviously the critical factor, but unless a competitor can also go fast, he has little chance of winning.

Here the faster route is the more dangerous and you must decide whether it is worthwhile taking the chance.

carefully. Also tracks that appear completely clear when you are walking round, all too often are blocked on the day with spectators, or gates are padlocked, or an open field becomes a car park. If short cuts are being used they must be double-checked on the day itself and a friend stationed to clear the way if necessary.

Any particular advice on water obstacles?

Always check the depth. Spreads over deep water must be jumped clean, but sometimes a fence designed to be cleared can in fact be ridden through. The 22nd and last fences at Mexico were good examples, and if Jane Bullen on Our Nobby had crept slowly through these two streams, as several riders did, she would have avoided two falls. One year at Burghley, the water jump was extremely shallow one side and quite deep on the other, so the wise rider jumped the shallow end.

I think you should get into the water yourself, clad in swimming wear or fishing waders depending on the season, and check the bottom to see what sort of going it is.

How about the second walk round? What different things are you looking for?

Before the second walk round, the rider must sit down and consider the course as a whole. He has studied the fences individually but he must now think of them in relation to each other. For instance, a succession of fairly fast, straightforward fences can result in both horse and rider getting careless, often standing off too far and frequently going too fast. The rider must also think how tiring the course is, due to the going, like hills and twistiness of route; also if you have a late draw, then you must consider how the course will alter after the other competitors have been over it.

The rider will set out on his second walk round, checking his intended route and all the way round he will be deciding how many yards to right or left of each tree or marker he will pass. He must make constant checks on his approaches and the experienced rider finds landmarks all the way to enable him to take the shortest and quickest routes over and away from each fence, and the best approach to the next. These landmarks should be clearly visible and permanent.

Ideally one looks for high objects like pylons, telegraph poles, buildings, church spires, chimneys or trees. If you use trees, it's advisable to be able to recognise them, as I discovered at Badminton one year when a rider was aiming for a beech instead of an ash and could have taken completely the wrong line.

How about the time of day? Is this a factor?

Knowing your place in the draw, you should whenever possible do the second walk round

All decisions as to what to
do when in trouble must
have been thought out in
advance. It is essential to
study all possibilities and to
have made the decisions on
your intended escape route.

at approximately the same time as when you will be riding. You must consider where the sun is going to be, should it decide to shine. Some fences alter tremendously with the change from morning to afternoon light. The fifth fence at Munich caused problems when the sun blinded the horses as they came out of the dark, but only three competitors were affected because they jumped the fence within the half hour that the sun was in that particular position.

At Wylye, several years ago, we had three successive falls at a fence where the sun was a problem in late afternoon, and there is now an alternative let-out to give riders a chance.

Do crowds represent a major problem?

Very much so. A lonely rope or string on walk-round day can become a throng of colourful and constantly moving bodies, often with umbrellas, and all these things can distract a horse during the last vital strides of approach. Whenever possible, the chosen route should give an obvious route away on landing, preferably down a track, between lines of spectators or through the trees.

The two Vicarage corners at Badminton 1977 were good examples of this. The first, although making one jump instead of three, was asking the horse to jump apparently straight into the crowd, thus you had the risk of a horse dropping his hind legs and landing short. The second V jump, although demanding great accuracy, showed far more daylight on the route away. At the Powderham trials there was a fence that was jumped towards a railway line and this was very disconcerting if there was a train passing at that time. This proved a difficult distraction to forecast because not many riders had a train timetable!

Should you have decided on your route by the time you do the second walk round?

The rider should set out on his second walk round knowing what lies ahead so he is now in a position to make his final decisions. Although he aims at a quick round, saving every possible second, a refusal or a fall usually removes all chances of a prize, so his dash must be tempered with discretion. Speed is certainly important, but the rider must remember that he doesn't want an exhausted horse for those all-important last few jumps.

The way one fence is jumped has a bearing on how the next is jumped. A big drop which jars the back and legs will make even the boldest of horses cautious at the next drop. Because of this, a quick way through an alternative involving an uncomfortable landing might be wisely avoided if the next fence is similar without any choice. Again, sometimes there is a choice of over water or through it, so if a difficult water splash comes later in the course, it can be a good opportunity to get the horse's feet wet.

Above all, at the second viewing the rider must decide his first choice of route with the prime consideration of saving time and effort. One jump takes less out of a horse than two and is almost always quicker, particularly if it takes a direct route to-

The final score will depend far more on the time not wasted jumping the obstacles and getting away on the best possible line to the next.

wards the next obstacle. The way you get away from a fence is of vital importance if you wish to make good time.

Do you consider alternatives during the second walk round?

Yes, and all alternatives must be carefully walked. When a rider has decided on his intended route, he should also be certain of his second and third choices, and it is essential that changes of plan should never be made unless the alternative has been thoroughly walked.

Corners appeal to some and not to others. Basically they are a test of obedience and accuracy, but as they always involve a considerable spread the horse must have impulsion, and a big corner on a tired horse at the end of a long course can sometimes mean taking an unnecessary risk. Deciding the line at a corner is extremely important as accuracy to an inch is essential; having chosen the exact point over which to jump, a suitable landmark must be selected to give you the right line.

Many alternatives, and some straight fences, demand taking one or more elements on the angle to find the best line through and away. It is essential that the horse has been properly taught to jump on a diagonal and learnt the vital key of straightness. The trained horse maintains the line on which he is put at all times, unless asked to change it. All top riders know that any deviation from straight must be corrected instantly whether in a competition or schooling. The horse who jumps frequently to left or right of his line is certain to end up getting himself into trouble, and with such horses it is wiser to avoid corners; even six inches off course can be a disaster.

It is essential that riders remember that the angling of obstacles requires obedience and accuracy and, where spreads are involved, may be dangerous. Wide parallels should never be taken on the angle; nor should bullfinch obstacles, as even a slight angle on the latter will cause the fence to look like a completely impenetrable barrier with no daylight visible. Jumping on the angle onto slopes and into water is always taking a risk. Riders must never forget that hitting a fence when jumping diagonally is much more likely to cause a fall and, for this reason, the angling of fences towards the end of a long course needs care, as a tired horse finds it more difficult to keep his feet than a fresh one.

Are there any special competition rules about multiple fences?

The rules differ for one-, two- or three-day events, and you must know about the

Deciding the exact line on a corner is extremely important and accuracy to the inch is essential.

penalty zones. The French rider at the Montreal Olympics who circled between two fences to try to rebalance his horse after a fall and two refusals, although then jumping clear was not only eliminated himself but the team also. At Bromont also, a Mexican rider accumulated three refusals by persisting in re-jumping element A of the 10th obstacle after refusals at part B, although it was far easier to jump B alone, having successfully negotiated A.

All decisions as to what to do in trouble must also have been worked out in advance. Even the best horses can make a slight error over the first elements and be forced to a refusal at the second. Then comes the vital decision as to whether to retake the entire obstacle, use a new approach altogether, or use the let-out provided. Such let-outs are quite frequently not even noticed by riders during their walk round or worse still even ignored.

It is essential to study all possibilities and to have made definite decisions on any intended escape routes. Faced with a completely unexpected refusal or fall, the flustered rider often makes a hurried re-approach without sufficient thought; but thought wastes vital seconds, and decisions like that have to be made in advance.

What points are you looking for in the third walk round?

The second walk round must be the "decision making" round and if a rider has any doubts, he should have another look before embarking on the final, and exact, walking of the course. I think most riders like to talk to a trainer or knowledgeable friend, memorising the exact track to be ridden and how to ride it every inch of the way. Such things like pace, speed, direction, the landmarks to head for, where to rebalance, where to steady, where to gallop on, where to change the whip to the other hand, where to check the stop-watch, etc., must be carefully thought through so as to clarify every tiny point. Even thinking through the course last thing at night can be a great help, and hopefully produces pleasant dreams rather than nightmares.

The rider should choose a time when few people are around for the final walk round; frequently early morning or evening is the best time. Above all, he should do his final trip alone, so that he really concentrates and imagines himself actually riding the course. It even pays to run the tricky and twisting bits where quick thinking is going to be needed.

The rider should feel on that final walk that the route he is taking will enable him to achieve a rhythm and regularity of speed,

with a minimum of checking and shortening the stride in front of the fences, which can tire the horse and slow the time; also avoid sharp and violent increases of pace which are equally tiring and likely to cause leg trouble. The aim is to jump each obstacle with the minimum of effort, combined with the shortest possible route. With regard to height of fences, it often pays to carry a tape measure on the first or second course-viewing to check heights and spreads, as cleverly constructed fences often produce many optical illusions.

As regards the checking of stop-watches, a few riders like to measure the course to know the quarter, half and three-quarter points. However, although this is a tremendous help on the steeplechase phase, for the cross-country it can merely be misleading as, in spite of theoretically aiming for a regular speed and rhythm, certain obstacles and certain sections of every course will have to be taken slowly, while other parts obviously provide galloping stretches.

To win the competition, jumping the fences is obviously the critical factor but a

competitor has little chance of success unless he can also go fast. However, just speed on the flat can be very deceptive and the final score will depend far more on the time not wasted jumping the obstacles and getting away on the best possible line to the next. All this comes back to careful, thorough and intelligent walking of the course.

Alternative fences must be looked at very thoroughly.

When walking round you must not only take careful note of the jump but you must also take into account the crowds who will assemble on the day of the actual event. The ropes on the right might be holding back spectators complete with umbrellas, children and dogs.

Chapter 2

The First Obstacle and Start
Aly Adsetts

To me the vital thing about the start and the first obstacle is that it probably establishes the rhythm for the rest of the round. Would you agree?

When I go through the start, I go slightly slower. I try to get in a rhythm approaching the first fence, but I'm not going at the pace I hope to be going the rest of the round. If you make a muck-up of the first two or three fences, the horse feels uncomfortable and will be a little bit on edge the rest of the way.

Do you slow down and "show jump" the first fence?

For the steeplechase you've got to be quick off the mark because the time is so vital and therefore over the first fence I'm very nearly going the speed I'm going to go all the way round. At the start of any part of the three-day event course, the steeplechase or the cross-country, you've got to tell your horse that you mean business. It's not just "Here we go for a nice canter round". They've got to be on the ball.

What physically do you do before the start?

In the box when the man says 20 seconds, 10, 9, 8, 7, etc., from that time onwards one shortens one's reins ready to kick the minute he says "Go!"

What advice would you give to a complete novice who is competing in their first or second one-day event?

It's definitely important where the first fence is sited. The competitors' box for the cross-country is probably near the show jumping arena and the first fence is out in the country, so a novice horse that is young and green doesn't have a great desire to leave the crowds.

I have seen first fences ride badly because people forget that a novice horse has got to go, and whether they are going away from other horses or towards them makes a terrific difference. You want a bit of speed, but it's more important to make sure they're going strong in the hand.

What would you advise a novice rider to do when he's had a bad first fence?

I would always give the horse one with the stick, making sure that when I gave it one it really accelerated away from me, and if it didn't, I would give it another one just to make jolly sure it was going forward. Sometimes if they are leaning to one side or hanging back, you give them one with the stick and they don't take much notice, so you've got to be prepared to give them a couple. You've got to get them going a bit stronger, accelerating forwards, so you can collect them up a bit more for the second fence.

Let's say one is a very good rider and you're bringing on a young horse. Do you have a different technique if you are setting out for a fast time?

It depends where the first fence is. Sometimes you get them very near the start and other times they're quite a long way off. If it's a long way and you're out to try and win,

Kinlet A rather untidy start and she looks as if she is running towards the left, and having a bit of trouble trying to turn it.

I hold my horse away from the actual start line as long as possible because I find the waiting gets the horse keyed up and in a frenzy.

First Fence at Wellesbourne Rider and horse are a bit sloppy. The rider has given the horse one with the stick which was probably the right thing to do. Reins are slightly long and horse is off the bit, and rider should have a stronger contact.

Not enough "oomph" at the start.

29

I think you've got to get hold of the horse at the start and get into a rhythm as quickly as you can from the word go.

Let's move on from novice events to intermediate, and talk about a first steeplechase. Would you recommend extended fast work and practice over steeplechase fences, or simply do them as and when they come along?

I have never schooled any of my horses over steeplechase fences. They get their cantering work regularly up until the three-day event, so, hopefully, when it comes to doing the steeplechase, they're ready to go. They feel good, they want to go, and a steeplechase fence is a very inviting fence, so if the horse doesn't want to take such a fence at speed, you've probably got a slightly chicken horse who shouldn't be entered for a three-day event in the first place.

It's very annoying to drop time on a steeplechase. How do you establish pace and then judge that you've got it right?

I suppose I've done it enough times to know, but I remember when I first started three-day eventing, it was a terrific help watching others ride on a steeplechase. One realised that one had to go all the way and not take it easy. When you ride a steeplechase course, you have got to keep up the rhythm all the way to complete the course on time. The horse must be properly fit, and the rider too.

Do you think riders spend enough time getting fit?

A lot of people have jobs during the week and only ride weekends which might be hampering for them, but I think you get so many schools of thought with novices. Some people, on their first event, don't want to push their horses too hard in the steeplechase but I think that if you're going anywhere in this sport, you've got to be more professional about it. My attitude is that it's costing me an absolute fortune to go eventing anyway, and I'm not going to my first event not to push the horse as hard as I can over the steeplechase. It means that if I'm spending three months getting my horse ready with all the work and the hours on the road, and the money to train, and the money to go to other events, it's ridiculous to say it doesn't matter if it has fifteen time penalties. I reckon the training should be properly done and since nowadays you can't event horses that are too young because of the restrictions, then if your horse is old enough, it should be ready to *go*.

What sort of work do you do leading up to the first novice event? What would be a typical work programme to ensure that you get round at the speed you wanted to go?

If I've got a completely novice horse given to

me to be evented that season, I do quite a bit of hacking over country where you can give it a canter and a trot so that you get it fit. I would then go to as many hunter trials as possible so that it sees all the fences. I would also school over cross-country fences where you don't have to go over at speed but can, if necessary, trot over things like little coffins and ditches. I don't think I've ever taken any of my horses at cross-country speed prior to going round at their first event, because the first event I take them to, I never go out to win as such. I take them round steadily so that their mental impression of their first event is "Isn't this fun!" I find the next time out they're raring to go. I think this is important because to get a good pace across country, you must trust your horse and have faith in him and make him believe everything's all right and there aren't going to be any falls. You set up a totally competent picture, and I find you can ride at a good speed and build up a lovely rhythm.

One reads so often that half the entries at novice events aren't really fit enough to compete. Do you have a laid-out programme of work, or do you make it up as you go along?

I usually start novices off with the target of the Tidworth Three-Day Event in the spring, in which case I start getting the horse ready on 1 January for an event which takes place in May. If I was doing only one-day events instead of three-day, I would still start in January, bearing in mind that the first events are in March. I don't have a fixed programme but I have a sort of programme worked out in my head. Horses must have a certain amount of hacking out and road work, so one day you have a long hack and the next day a short hack and a canter. The next day they might have a bit of schooling, but if you have a problem and you go on schooling a long time, then they don't get hacked out.

Do you err on the side of more work rather than less?

I remember once telling some riders of my own programme just before the three-day event at Wylye when I'd hacked out for two and a half hours on the road, and then had a twenty-five-minute steady canter, followed by five minutes fast. This was part of the final preparation just before the event, and the other riders were absolutely fascinated, they thought this was a tremendous amount of work. But I am a great believer in getting horses really fit. I do a lot of trotting on the road—it does not do them any harm at all— and they are constantly having canters either in schooling work or on hacks out or just round the outside of a field. Horses keep a lot sounder, they're fit through and through, and they're not carrying any excess weight. I personally don't do any hunting because I haven't lived in good hunting country, but I think it would be difficult to hunt through the winter, rest them a little, and then event them.

What is your procedure before the cross-country when you have finished the roads and tracks? What happens before you go up to the starter?

When you get back to the box, the vets will want to have another look at them. I try and arrive twelve minutes before the start rather than the ten which are allowed and I take the saddle off and give the horse a good wipe down. I don't take the bridle off their faces but they are given a nice cool wipe so that they feel refreshed in the inside of their mouth. They are then walked round with a sweat rug on, and the saddle is put on again, about three or four minutes before we go. I don't actually do this myself because I like to have a quick look round to learn what sort of tales of death and destruction there have been, and if there's a television set I obviously go and have a look. I very seldom have a drink because I don't feel like anything.

Do you actually set out to gain any intelligence of what's gone before? Do you have a friend or helper to tell you what's happening?

Yes, I do. I always want to know about the fences I'm most worried about. This year at Badminton there were two lovely examples of that, the Lake and the Vicarage fences, because there were two parts to each and there were time-saving routes. I wanted to know if anybody had ridden the quick way and was it all right. Not that it makes an awful lot of difference, but just that I like to know. I don't change what I planned to do because I've seen somebody do something else. It's just that if you see somebody go the way you're going to go, it's very encouraging if they do it very well!

Taking courses in general, both here and abroad, would you always expect the first fence to be straightforward?

Every course builder wants their course to ride well. Courses are meant to be interesting and cause problems, but you don't want anything ghastly to happen. You don't want a bad first fence where people have errors, because that's not what it's all about; you want people to start well and then it's up to them to cope with what's ahead.

I've seen some good people fall at the first fence, and I've seen a lot of run-outs, especially in one-day events, but usually you get a nice first fence to get people started. You could have an error if you rode out of the box like fury trying to break the course record or something. All fences at Badminton and Burghley are big, but if you're used to three-day events, you should be able to cope.

Brigstock A good start with plenty of enthusiasm. They've taken the middle of the fence, horse's ears are forward and rider's hands are quite level.

Chapter 3

The Drop Fence
Diana Thorne

Do you do anything different for a drop fence?

If my horse is a free, forward-going horse, I usually have short reins and I have him balanced. But when I'm coming up to a drop fence, I've got to have a longer rein and at the same time I've got to keep a tight hold. If it's an enormous drop down, I've got to be able to hold him on landing or he may trip. If it's a combination drop fence and quarry like at Badminton, you've got to have balance and keep them looking forward to the next part. But probably the hardest part is the actual landing, being able to hold them and keep them together. Most riders lean back a little as they go down the drop and that's probably correct, but I personally always lean forward slightly. I keep my foot well in the stirrup and I keep my legs on. One must be able to slip the reins in order to lean back so you don't get yanked over the horse's head!

Sometimes I have a different technique for different horses. I'm schooling a novice at the moment, and I have to kick to make it look and then pop down over the drop. But even so, I'm usually leaning forward slightly. With an advanced horse, I just slow them down as I approach the drop and get them into a nice bouncy stride.

Princess Anne at Osberton You can gallop over this one and it's quite a nice feeling, but here the hind legs have got twisted. Princess Anne is leaning back and she's practically holding the buckle. But she's got her legs well forward and can get herself out of trouble.

Badminton Everything right. Heels down, toes up. Horse is jumping nicely out from the fence, and she's going with the horse. Classic position.

Double Ski Drop at Badminton Never go into a drop fence crookedly. This rider's doing all right but the horse is slightly askew.

Good landing. Feet well in the stirrups and legs are forward. Leaning back slightly but otherwise good position and he's nice and straight.

Second part of Badminton's Double Ski Drop Rider is much too far forward when he should be more upright. Legs are back which is wrong.

Off fore caught the top of the fence and it's going to be a fall. Nothing rider can do now.

A proper turnover.

Osberton No wonder this rider looks happy, because he's done almost everything right. Horse is going forward, rider's got his legs forward, he's well in the stirrup and he looks as if he's balanced. His hands are a bit high but you can't really complain about that.

Corbridge I remember this one at Corbridge. Normally for this horse, I wear a crossed noseband and it happened to break just before the fence. About four strides away the horse suddenly got away from me and instead of popping down the bank, he took an enormous big jump. We landed about 20 ft. right over the bank, onto the flat at the bottom. I'm not doing anything radically wrong, I'm sitting right and going forward, but I had not got him balanced at the top of the fence. I remember the landing because it jarred my injured shoulder which was still strapped up from a previous fall and very painful. It was a lovely feeling flying through the air if only I hadn't had a bad shoulder.

I was the only one who jumped clean over the fence and the drop. Most riders just popped over the fence onto the bank.

What advice would you give a rider who was training a novice to go over drop fences?

If you've done a season's hunting, you've probably jumped a few drops without realising it. You don't want to practise too often with big drops because it can be a strain on the forelegs. You want to get the horse used to going forward and the best way to practise is up and down a quarry, because once he's started to go down, he's got to keep going down. Try and jump small drop fences whenever possible, but unfortunately they are few and far between.

For the novice it is better to jump drops at a trot to begin with, letting him take a look, and then pop down. Don't do an extravagant jump. When he knows a little more, canter, and approach the drop with more "go" but at a slower speed. Keep a light contact on the rein, maintain balance and allow the head and neck to stretch. He should try not to jump too high because that only exaggerates the drop. The horse must always be kept straight.

Cirencester This is a good example of the other method of taking drop fences which I personally don't subscribe to. It probably depends what sort of horse it is and I can't say there's anything wrong. She's on a long rein, I think it's Lorna Sutherland, and she's leaning back. It may depend on the horse because if it's a bit sticky she can boot it forward.

Generally with drop fences, do you think a forward going-on position is more effective than a safety-first position?

If you're holding on to the buckle there's always trouble on landing, especially if the horse trips. But if you're leaning slightly forward and you've got your legs forward, you should be all right.

In the water at Osberton It looks as if the horse jumped crooked, almost as if he didn't want to go into the water. Perhaps he tried to run out. You must go straight, especially into a water fence. I'm glad it wasn't me; it looks very nasty.

Badminton This rider's got everything right. She's got good contact and the legs in the right place. She's going with the horse and it's important to be with the horse and not behind.

Same drop fence at Badminton from a different angle This rider's got behind. The horse probably hesitated before taking off, and her legs have shot back slightly. Looks as if she's in for a bad landing. Reins a bit loose.

Batsford I believe the rider broke her wrist at this fence, but we don't know if the horse broke anything. I should think she went too slowly, because the horse obviously hasn't jumped out properly. Horse must have caught its knee on the top rail.

Are there any particular drop fences that still give you nightmares?

This year at Badminton, I was very worried about the quarry fence. It wasn't so much a nightmare as a worry because I couldn't make up my mind which side of the wall to jump. If you jumped on the left, it was fairly straight, but you'd have to come out before you went up.

I intended to jump the wall on the right so I'd have more time, but I was so worried about what the drop would do to me because my horse is very quick on landing. I wasn't so worried about the actual ramp because mine's a very free-going horse, always going forward, and if you've got enough momentum, he just pops over. But if you've got a very sticky, slow horse, you've got to have a lot of impulsion, a lot of power, to get up and over. Having decided beforehand to go right, I changed my mind and went left mainly because everyone else was going left and it was less of a risk.

In the Farmyard at Everdon The rider looks very determined to get on with it. There's a left turn coming up and they're already on the correct line and they seem to have everything right. Very good.

Chapter 4

Jumping into the Dark
Rachel Bayliss

Does jumping into darkness create any particular problems?

Yes, absolutely. It's not so much the problem with the fences. It's more a state of mind. Many of the fences are actually quite straightforward and there aren't that many combination fences. Usually you get the straightforward big black log pile with a flat landing going up an alley way into the wood. Having walked the course beforehand, you know it's straight after landing, so about sixty yards before take off you persuade yourself that it's just a straightforward jump.

But suppose you're going from bright sunlight into a black nothingness?

From sixty yards, the horse can't see where he's got to go. So you've got to have the attitude of mind to say "Now come here, chap! Here's something different. Pay attention!"

How do you do that?
You just take a pull and engage them a little more for a couple of strides to get their attention. More than you'd do for an ordinary fence. You must get their attention, get their hocks a little more engaged and say "Come on now, behave yourself."

The stream at Llanfechain Here at Llanfechain you've got a different sort of problem. The stream is hidden from the horse's view and so is the fence. So you come bowling across this lovely flat field, all long and free and happy with your horse's ears forward, and it looks easy. But if you don't sit down ten strides away from this dip and get his attention, the horse is going to be very unbalanced as he sees into the dip. So you want him very engaged and attentive and waiting for something different, and it's fine, and over you go. If you get your approach right to these sort of fences, then it's all right. But if you come along too fast and go down unbalanced, then the horse is all in a panic. Because suddenly you've got water and drops and darkness, and Help! there's a fence. You've got to explain what's happening to the animal because he can't see from a long way off.

5-foot drop into the woods at Earl Soham Now this looks sticky but it would be absolutely typical. The fence is your average "interesting-into-woods-type fence". Lots of trees and probably a drop on the other side, 4 or 5 feet perhaps. You can imagine this rider hammering in at 90 miles an hour, but without getting the horse's hocks underneath it and without getting its attention. Suddenly the horse gets a stride away and says "Oh Christ, what am I going to do? There are trees there and that's a drop and nobody's told me anything!" And, of course, he hesitated. Then you can imagine them circling back and getting it all together and coming in with nice impulsion. But it's a bit late really as this time the horse has had a proper look at the woods and knows it's all right.

45

At the exact moment of darkness, can you expect resistance?

Not if you've got their attention beforehand. About ten strides away, you would say "Wake up! Here's something a bit different. You've got to do as you're told and there's a wood coming up."

What advice would you give a novice eventer who has problems going into woods?

Get them used to changes of light and don't try them over fences to start with. Canter across fields where there are plenty of dark places, like hollows or big trees. Get young horses used to cantering from bright sunlight into shade. Then practise in the woods; usually there are plenty of woods about. But really for any type of eventing, it's absolutely vital to walk the course beforehand and you must remember what comes after the fence.

How do you mean?

You nearly always have to turn left or right after entering a wood and it's important to get the correct line. If you're jumping a fence in the middle of a field, it doesn't matter if you're four feet to the left or right, and you can start thinking about the next fence when you're still on the top. But in a wood with nasty big trees in the way, you've got to be terribly accurate.

Really, you have to be accurate to within a yard, especially if there are other fences in the woods. Get your line right in plenty of time and know which way you're going to land and which tree you're going to go round. This is pretty basic for any fence, but you must be much more careful when there's a change of light and you can't see ahead. You must have that little bit more attention and get your horse more engaged so it isn't quite so much of a shock. That's it really. You must prepare him so he doesn't get too much of a shock.

In that split second when you go from sunlight into darkness, how quickly can the horse's eyes get used to the change?

Quite quickly. It's not really a problem. The biggest problem is the surprise and shock element and really that's a matter of attention.

How about jumping out of woods? Is that a problem?

Jumping out is a piece of cake because the horse can see where it's going. If you're coming out of woods and there's a nice open field in front of you, then the horse pricks up his ears and off we go.

Can you think of any fences on any of the courses you've competed on that have been particularly nasty?

Not really. They're normally straightforward if you get the line right. The ones that give the most trouble are the ones with drops. They cause trouble because people come in too fast and try to get over by speed and not by impulsion. There are some nasty fences going into woods, usually stiff posts and rails with drops, or a ditch and rail with drops, that cause trouble and falls. But the usual fault is going in too fast because the rider is worried that the horse may not go in at all.

Would you say going too fast is the classic fault?

Always.

In eventing generally, how much do you think is talent on the part of the rider, and how much is the horse?

I would think it was nearer 90% horse and 10% rider. And most of the rider's talent is natural talent.

How do you mean?

They just seem to do the right things automatically.

Do you think once a rider has demonstrated some sort of talent, then it's going to be the quality of the horse that makes it come good?

There are a few riders, very few, that can produce horse after horse but normally it's one person to one horse. You see them for a while and then they disappear, or sometimes they bring novices on and you see them again. Once you've passed the novice stage, it's the talent of the horse that's most important.

So you either spend a lot of money, or you keep searching or you're just lucky.

Most of us are lucky. We find a good horse to learn on and then muddle on with others until we find another. You need a combination of intelligence and ability. You get wild horses that can jump over the moon, and intelligent horses that are so clever that they can't be bothered. And after all, why should they? To get ability and intelligence in the right mixture is very rare indeed.

How did you get into eventing? In America they have about seven grades of competition and you can progress gradually from one to the other. But in England it's different.

Some people get a terrible shock at their first novice event. It's a lot bigger than they thought. The lucky ones are those who come up through Pony Club events. Then from Pony Club events to Junior and then into the Open. That's the best way. But there are many people who buy horses and go straight from hunter trials to an open novice event and it's a terrible shock!

Problems at Lockerley Now this rider's got a lot of problems. He's taken the jump straight and looks as if he's going slap into that bush. I would have come in on an angle to go left or right or whatever the line is. You can see why the line is so important. He's also riding very short.

Going well at Burghley Now this rider's done everything right. It looks very nice. She's taken the fence absolutely straight on but you can see there is open space ahead. The horse is very alert, you can tell by the ears and the face. She probably sat down a few strides before the fence, got a bit of extra impulsion, and everything's gone beautifully.

Chapter 5

The Coffin

Jane Starkey

Do you have any special thoughts, or techniques, when approaching a coffin?

I think one of the most important things is to let the horse see as much of the problem as he can. With a coffin you've got to let the horse see the job in hand and he probably won't be able to see the ditch at the bottom if the distance or the gradient into the middle is very steep, but he will probably be able to work out a lot more than one gives him credit for. At most of the coffins on the big courses you turn into them, and you can turn in too short. If they're a really brilliant horse and they do just what you say, they'll go. But you're going to have a far better ride through, and the horse won't drop a leg in

the ditch or pitch you up its neck, if he has time to see and balance himself before going into the fence.

What about speed of approach?

I don't worry so much about speed, as much as line. I am very definite about the line I take into a fence and I take a more generous line into a coffin. I take a slower route, not slower in speed, but a slower route into coffins than any other fence on the course. The speed depends entirely on the type of coffin. There are some coffins which are flat and don't shoot you down and up a precipice, and you can take these flat coffins at a normal speed. Obviously you've got to

Bucklebury This lady rider was not exactly prepared for the horse to take off. But the horse was going forward with interest and no doubt the two sorted themselves out. Good example of a coffin being a problem for the rider rather than a technical problem for the horse.

Jane Starkey at the Double Coffin at Burghley The double coffin at Burghley has two ditches with a differing distance between them. You could jump it on the right where it was definitely a bounce, or you could jump it slightly to the left where there was possibly room for a stride. I took it nearer the left because Topper is a short-striding horse and if he took the extra stride, he would land well up the bank. The bank is much steeper than it appears in the photograph.

The double coffin was a new idea and the main problem with this one is that the approach is downhill and one is inclined not to check the horse until it's too late.

collect the horse and get it together when you make the approach and you must have impulsion. Above all it's impulsion rather than speed that you simply must have.

How do you create this impulsion? Do you have any particular way of shortening up?

I do much the same thing for everything. I just generally tell the horse to pay attention. I like to ride my horses very firm in the hand.

But before a fence I will increase the contact and give them a couple of kicks and perhaps a slap on the neck and shorten them, and say "Pay attention." I don't often see a stride, and I try not to see a long one because I've come unstuck riding into coffins with too long a stride. For that matter, horses don't take any combinations very well off too long a stride. They really want to be shortened up with you sitting down. As long as you're on a shortened stride with impulsion they will get through it. But if you're on a long flat stride with nothing, you get over the first part, then you may land in the ditch. Or if you get over the first two parts, you may get in a muddle over the last bit. But if you've got the impulsion and you're on a shortened stride, you should be able to get through.

Another prime rule is that although you are aware of the first two elements, you ride for the last. It's like the old saying when you're teaching a-ten-year old to jump his first pole. "Throw your heart over the fence and you'll get over". I was taught very early in the Pony Club that when you want to jump combinations, ride for the last part and you'll get through.

Nigel Tabor on Pirate at Brigstock A flat coffin with no gradients leading in and out of the ditch. A nice coffin which you can ride through in your stride and shouldn't present any big problems even though both the fences are quite substantial.

Talking about stride, I find both my horses, Acrobat and Topper, have seen the stride long before I have, and I very often see the wrong one anyway. Horses are pretty good at judging their own stride.

When you walk the course beforehand, do you measure the strides between the different elements?

When I walk a combination or coffin-type fence, I always stride it, but I am not very brilliant on the striding thing. I say to myself, "That looks like one stride, or two", but they can be extremely deceptive. You've only got to watch six horses jump one coffin and you'll see many variations. More important, I think, is when you land after the first part that you're not left behind or sitting on the horse's ears. You must, hopefully, be in the centre of gravity, still in contact with the front end, sitting still, and accept the fact that the horse might take more strides than you thought. Once you're committed, I don't think there's a lot you can do to influence it one way or the other, unless it suddenly says "Don't think I'm going to go on", and you can jolly well say go!

I know you can be more forceful but I never try and tell a horse to put in two strides here or three strides there. They usually know better than I do.

Would you say hunting is useful to achieve cleverness on the part of the horse?

I've only hunted in Warwickshire but a horse can learn an awful lot about how to look after itself. It won't learn how to canter on the right leg or how to jump a coffin, but there are a lot of ditches and fences out hunting and a horse soon learns to look after itself. I would certainly advise hunting if you live in the right part of the world and you can afford it. But it's expensive and it can be dangerous. Acrobat was nearly written off last season.

Hunting is very good experience for a promising young horse because it will learn a tremendous lot about going forward, looking after itself, or getting used to crowds. But if you live in a hunt where all they do is trot round the roads, then I would say spend your money on lessons or stay with someone who will let you jump their cross-country fences.

How would you introduce a horse to coffins?

Find somewhere where there's a plain ditch to start with and practise over that. When the horse was happy, I'd put a pole a distance away on the landing side and teach it to jump the ditch and the pole. Then put the pole before the ditch, and practise that. Then put poles each side of the ditch, and make it increasingly difficult.

Coffins are something it's well worth spending some time on, however good you think your horse is. Just because you've got a good hunter, don't think he'll go sailing round his first novice event. You don't have to go to a lot of trouble to build a coffin. First find a ditch and put a couple of cavaletti either side.

Can we discuss coffins you have come to love or hate?

Basically, I don't dislike coffins or combinations because the type of horse I've got at the moment finds combinations easy. The only coffin-type fence I had trouble at was

Mark Phillips at Burghley
He jumped in very nicely, and he jumped over the ditch very nicely. Most horses put in a stride between the ditch and the fence, but Persian Holiday being a great big, long-striding horse, decided to bounce it. Having decided to bounce it, suddenly he started to touch down again with a hind leg, giving Mark no chance of staying on. Mark was very unlucky.

I think it's an example of how a coffin can sometimes be a problem for a big, long-striding horse. Neither of my horses is particularly long-striding, they're fairly short-striding and sort of cat-like, and they're fairly athletic. So for my horse it was one stride, over, one stride, out. And it was just right. This is a difficult coffin because there's a slope down, quite a large ditch which you must jump rather than step, and a tricky slope up to the second fence.

52

Fiona Moore at the Sunken Footpath at Badminton This coffin is an absolute stinker. The first part in was very high and the ground ran right away from you. The ditch at the bottom is nothing but it was quite steep to get out. Basically, once you got in you were going to get out and I rode into it very firmly. I went into it fairly strongly, he landed, took one stride, jumped the ditch, took a stride and jumped out.

Fiona's going well here. She's looking ahead and not into the ditch. She's sitting tight, holding onto the front end and the horse looks to have the whole thing summed up.

Heustridge An example of a nice kind coffin. No precipices leading in and out of the ditch and plenty of space. The sort of coffin you might like to school over.

at Bramham, which was basically a sunken road, with a post and rails on each side. It was in the days when Topper didn't really accept the bit and didn't do as he was told. I came in with a nice long stride and I kicked for it and he said "You must be joking" and just switched off. I confused speed with impulsion. He was on too long a stride with no impulsion to jump that particular fence. Whether coffins are favourite fences or not favourite fences, they create problems for the rider rather than technical problems for a horse. I think there can sometimes be technical problems like the coffin at the 1973 Badminton. I didn't walk the course very seriously but the coffin appeared to be short for long-striding horses. But usually the coffin is a problem for the rider, not the horse.

Coming out of the coffin at Burghley.

Chapter 6

Steps and Banks
Jane Holderness-Roddam

How do you deal with a step or a bank?

I think the most important thing is to get the impulsion to make it possible for the horse to do that big jump up, particularly if it's a series of steps, because they have to have the speed to keep on going up. It's easy enough to jump on to one big bank and off again but with steps you've got to be under control and still have the impulsion to keep going up. It's a combination of controlled speed and impetus.

How do you personally create impulsion?

It's a pulling together and collecting them up and getting their hocks underneath them, so that they can push themselves up the steps. I try and bunch them up by taking a slightly firmer pull. The idea is to get the horse bunched together.

Do you find a bank more difficult than an actual fence?

I think they're incredibly difficult to jump but the important thing is not to get too far away, otherwise you can't struggle with them. Get close and treat them as an ordinary fence rather than a bank. You've got to consider the bottom line and the top line and the way you're going, rather than thinking you're jumping up onto something.

Do you find that if you're jumping onto the top of something, your body position is in rather a safer position than jumping a fence?

No, because it's rather difficult to keep your balance when you're on top because the horse sort of suddenly stops. It's difficult to keep your balance the whole time so as not to unbalance the horse. You've got to keep your balance very carefully and never get behind the movement or you could find yourself in very serious trouble. You never quite know how a horse is going to react to jumping a bank, because sometimes they change legs on the top. Very often they can't see what's on the other side till they're right on top. There may be a ditch or something on the other side, and they'll put in an unexpected stride.

It depends a lot on your horse. It's a pleasure to ride over banks with an experienced horse, but with a horse that's not too sure of itself, you must expect it to have a problem and it's difficult to keep them balanced. It's even more difficult coming down the other side. You've got to push a little bit harder and brace yourself to be ready for the landing.

Lockerley Lack of impulsion caused the horse to come to an abrupt halt, and the approach may have been too slow. It's a difficult fence because the post and rails came before the rather artificial-looking steps, and the brightly-coloured ground may have distracted the horse.

Miss A. Thomson on Kay's Lea, Corbridge Jumping down comfortably but it's possible she might have her weight too far forward.

What do you look for when you're walking the course?

I look to see if there is a ditch before or after it. What type of bank it is on top and whether it's round or flat. Also the height, because this affects the speed. I look to see if there's anything likely to put the horse off its stride. You've got to take all these things into account. You've also got to be very conscious of the width of the steps because this affects the speed and decides whether or not you've got to bounce them. It's probably easier to bounce them if the steps are narrow enough. With the wider ones, it's quite difficult to keep the impulsion going because obviously as they go up, they're going to land a bit shorter each time, and unless the steps have been designed that way, you can find they're trying to put a stride in at the top.

Langston's Ladder If you take the shortest route, ensure you can both survive the consequences!

What about the Normandy bank at Badminton that has a fence right on top?

It jumps very well as long as you go fast enough and get well on to the top. One or two people in the early days discovered, to their cost, that they couldn't put a stride in on top, and came to very bad grief because they got too close to the rail taking off. I'm not sure how wide they are in feet but they're quite wide on top, so there's plenty of room to go fairly fast and get well on to them so you can jump straight off and out the other side. If you come too steeply on to that sort of fence, you're liable to overbalance. It's very important to be going on so that you jump out well the other side and land safely.

What about coming down? Is there a vital difference?

Again, the balance of yourself and the horse is the most vital part. This time you're bracing yourself down and it's almost a slide. You don't want to go too fast, it's better to go slowly so that they just step down and keep going collectedly forwards. If you've got your weight in the right position and keep yourself balanced, it's probably easier coming down than going up.

What advice would you give to a rider who wants to school his horse for banks and steps?

The trouble with banks and steps is that they do jar a horse so you don't want to practise them too much. Make sure your first introduction for the horse is a pleasant one, so you want to start on something simple. Be certain it's a good bank, not one that's likely to collapse, and it should be quite small to start with. Make the horse happy popping up and popping down and play with him a little bit, making sure you never catch him in the face. Gradually progress to one or two slightly bigger ones, but I don't think you want to school him over a full-size bank or anything. Remember it is a jar for the horse and obviously if you keep doing something like that, they're going to get a bit fed up. If you're having difficulty, go about once a week just to play about and get them used to the habit of popping up and balancing themselves, and popping down. Start with small steps, one or two steps down perhaps, and progress to a nice bank where you've room to move and canter off. But I wouldn't want to do too much.

Wendover Looks as if the horse has gone through very quickly but he may have changed legs coming down and just shot her straight out of the saddle. Horse might have pecked.

Badminton. Diana Thorne on The Kingmaker Diana gets ten out of ten for this one. This is the classic position and she's doing everything right, particularly with the legs.

Follow-my-leader at Goodwood. The Clearing Bank The most common cause of failure at this type of obstacle is going too slowly. This rider wasn't going nearly fast enough and the horse is stopping long before it got to the fence. This is a big fence at Goodwood and you need plenty of impulsion and speed to get on top. Then a bounce and over you go. If you're going too slowly you would certainly need to put in a stride, but if you go fast it jumps very well—straight on and straight off—which is the only way to jump these types of fences unless they're very wide on top.

There are certain types of bank where a bounce should occur, and it sounds difficult to get a horse used to the idea that it pops up and immediately down. Is this something that has to be taught or can you let it happen naturally?

Unfortunately, that's a very difficult type of fence and unless a horse is really ready I think a lot of good horses could easily be ruined by doing too many bounce fences before they are physically capable. Even putting five or six-year-olds, fully developed ones, over that type of fence is asking for an awful lot of trouble, and unless things go right, you would easily put them off for life. You've got to get them very, very collected and it's important to get them right back on their hocks.

The sort of athletic exercises that pure show jumpers go in for can be incredibly

useful, and it's something the eventer could do more of.

I have noticed in the last few years that there've been some interesting lengths of stirrup. Some people ride incredibly long going across country, with almost straight legs, whereas others are riding quite short. What's your view?

I assume those people riding long are doing so for security reasons, though personally I think the longer you are, the more unsafe you are because of lack of leverage. You're better being fairly short, though not too short. If you're long, there's too much that can flop forwards and backwards, whereas if you're a bit shorter it means you're closer to the horse and have more control.

In this category of fence, and we're talking

about steps and banks, what is the nastiest one you can remember?

The one I was most worried about, but actually caused no trouble at all, was at Badminton going into the quarry where you had to go up a bank and over a wall at the top. It looked absolutely impossible. But when I got there the horse jumped onto a slight lip on the bank and then over the wall without any trouble.

When you're walking the course, do you often come to the conclusion that something looks totally impossible but the horse actually goes like a bomb?

As you jump your fences over the years, you begin to realise that horses seem to manage to jump an amazing amount of fences that look difficult and they usually jump them very well. As you walk the course, it looks dreadful to start with but as you walk it more and more it begins to fall into place. If anything looks really difficult, I would always suggest that you don't worry about it or sit and stare at it for hours. Go away and then come back again, two or three times if necessary, and somehow it becomes less and less of a problem. By the time you actually ride it, it seems to be no problem at all.

Bramham Oh dear! Because it was a slopping take-off I don't think the horse realised it was a jump and tried to walk up it. She's done well to stay on as long as she has, but she's too far forward to survive and her leg is back. If you can push your leg forward, it helps to keep you braced.

Karen Russell on Roversnick You don't want to make a mistake coming down this sort of fence but Karen looks very happy about it. She's sitting very upright and is well braced for the landing.

In overseas competitions, do you find they build steps and banks in a different way?

I've only ridden in Mexico and there everything seemed very different, mainly because they're actually using different sorts of timber. We're very lucky here with our sleepers and our telegraph poles, but they are more apt to have birch poles which aren't nearly so solid looking and that always takes a bit of getting used to. There's no doubt about it that if something looks solid and strong, then the horses seem to jump it that much better because they respect it.

What's the biggest fence in this category that you've come across?

I think at Badminton in 1973—the Luckington Crossing—was probably the worst fence I've jumped. Also the quarry. And almost anything going uphill where you simply must have plenty of impulsion, whether it's a bank, step or just a ramp. I think people forget there is an awful lot of effort that goes into anything uphill. I think everybody's got to get a move-on over their fences and nowadays everybody is getting too show jumping conscious and apt to lose the cross-country approach altogether. It makes it much more difficult for the horse because if they're going too slowly, it's that much more effort. I try to get my horses

going in a rhythm the whole way round the course, because you should remember it is an endurance test and you don't want them to take too much out of themselves. If you can keep going in a rhythm then it should be easy to use your legs a little bit, and pull a little bit, without actually having to slow down or quicken up too much. You so often see people going flat out round the course and then about half a mile before a fence they're pulling and shoving and kicking and pushing and wasting hours of time. It shouldn't be necessary to do anything until the last two or three strides or so, where you should be able to push a little bit more to get them balanced.

Do you find you have to work hard on your own physical fitness?

Yes, very hard, because I don't ride all the time, but I think one's own fitness is as important as the horse's. Other than riding, I run and swim quite a lot to develop my breathing, and I find swimming under water particularly good. I keep fairly fit because, though it sounds stupid, you get terribly breathless going round a steeplechase course. I've seen people at Badminton fall over the last three or four fences when they're both exhausted and tired. The horse pecks a bit and the rider comes off, but had he been physically fit, he might have been able to haul himself up and keep going.

Cirencester Rider is well braced if anything goes wrong and her weight is fairly well back. She's giving the horse his head so they should be all right.

Cirencester Going fast but rider looks very well balanced though he hasn't got much contact with the horse's head.

Chapter 7

Spreads
Horst Karsten

When you are riding into a straightforward fence, how far out do you start to think about it?

For a triple bar or a spread fence, I would ride at a normal cross-country speed, quite fast, and I would sit down a little bit in the last three or four strides. I would not alter the speed of the horse too much, but have him a bit more in the hand. I let him find his own way into the fence without interfering, and encourage him to take off at the appropriate moment.

Do you look for a stride?

I've got a good eye for a stride, and I see it from quite a long way out. I really start to

Windsor They've taken the fence as near the tree as possible, which is the fastest and easiest way. Rider should be standing more in the stirrups, but they have jumped well.

Osberton Rider is perched too far forward so if the horse were to stumble, she would be pitched off. She is also riding too long.

get the horse together in the last three or four strides. If it's a triple bar, I let him find his own way; he must look at the fence and jump from the bottom pole rather than standing off.

What about the true parallel when you can't judge the take-off point?

I do pretty much the same thing only earlier. I wouldn't let the horse gallop on so fast and I would start preparing him about six or seven strides away. I don't try to check him but sit down and hold him together, slowing up a little but not so much that I lose my cross-country speed. If you haven't got a good pace, you have to start riding forward again in the last few strides and it's then that

Windsor This horse has a good shape over the fence and they are going at the right speed.

the horse tends to stand up a bit.

How about the landing?

If it's a jump going downhill, I tend to sit a little bit back, not backwards exactly, so that I can get the horse in the hand again. For the next four or five strides, I sit with the horse.

If it's a large spread, it might have jumped rather big over the fence and you've got to help a little on the landing. This can be difficult, especially if the take-off hasn't been very good and he has landed awkwardly. If you've got the horse between hand and leg, you can sit down over the next few strides and get it back into the proper tempo for cross-country galloping, so saving valuable seconds.

Windsor The horse has a bit of a hollow back but he's looking forward to the next fence. The rider is sitting quite well in the saddle, but the reins are too short and the bit is rather high in the horse's mouth. The hind legs have only just cleared the fence, and they probably approached too fast in a sort of steeplechase style.

What is the difference in cross-country technique between English riders and German or American?

The English riders do a lot of hunting and they do hunter trials and that sort of thing, whereas there is nothing like that in Germany. Here in Germany if a horse isn't good enough for show jumping, then it becomes an event horse, whereas in England it's the other way round; if it's not good enough for hunting it becomes a show jumper. English horses tend to be thoroughbreds, whereas in Germany we have more half-breeds, which are a heavier-built type of horse.

In England there is plenty of open countryside for galloping and the English riders are used to going fast. The English horses have a much "looser" cross-country gallop and the riders tend to give the horses more freedom in their heads. The English horses give their riders "a ride" across country whereas the German riders give their horses "a ride"!

We do a lot of dressage here in winter; practically the whole winter is spent indoors doing it. In England, most people spend the winter hunting, which is a totally different type of training.

Bucklebury She probably didn't see a stride and rode slower and slower into the fence until the horse just couldn't jump. To jump properly you've got to flow over. The rider hasn't helped very much and just sat there waiting for the horse to jump till it was too late.

Sandhurst Horse has taken off rather late. Rider is very tense and looking down which is not good. Horse can't use his head and neck properly and is likely to hit the edge of the jump.

Fenton Difficult to say what happened but they probably approached the fence too slowly so that the horse hadn't got the speed to go over. Rider should be sitting further back with longer reins.

Earl Soham The rider has ridden the horse into the fence and jumped it very well. Perhaps the rider's legs should be further back and she shouldn't be leaning so far up the horse's neck, but otherwise it's very good.

I understand you do some coaching for eventing. Do you specifically school over an obstacle such as a spread?

The rider must first learn a good cross-country rhythm and tempo, and he can practise that in a field with natural obstacles such as hedges and ditches. Once he has developed a cross-country rhythm and learned a natural technique, I start to coach him over the jumps.

I explain first of all that you've got to help the horse to a certain extent, and if you see a good stride going into a fence, then O.K., ride on to that stride. Don't just sit with the horse and hope that the horse will find its own way.

This is a better way to start than always telling a novice rider to be careful, hold back, you're not right for the fence. The novice must learn to keep the tempo flowing until one gets the idea of riding across country.

Goodwood Rider probably tried to help the horse too much, by checking the speed and trying to see a stride. They've got over at the second attempt but not too happily. Horse's forelegs are dangling. This is not a big fence and there should be no problems getting over.

Do you put the novice riders on experienced horses?

I think it's a good idea to put a young rider on a horse that is good enough and clever enough to help him, rather than put an inexperienced rider on an inexperienced horse.

Do you do a lot of show jumping training with your event horses?

The horse has got to learn to look at the fence, and find its own way and balance itself. I use quite small combination fences with various poles so that the horse has to keep looking and finding its way out. It's very important that the horse learns to pick up its forelegs, especially in cross-country.

Are there any fences in International competition that you remember as being particularly bad?

The second fence at Kiev was the most difficult fence I've ever ridden. It was dangerously built and a very unfair fence because it came so early on. If it had been later it would have ridden much better. It was a big fence and it was downhill with a big ditch underneath it. My horse, Sioux, came in at too much of an angle, put on the brakes and went to one side. He jumped it the second time, and I feel I was very lucky to get over.

What is the best way of getting over a really difficult fence like that?

Always try and go over the middle. When you are walking the course, pay a certain amount of attention to exactly what the dangers could be if you came in on the wrong stride. Don't check the horse but ride with your usual cross-country tempo.

Tidworth Rider is sitting too much in the middle of the saddle but she has given with her hands so she should be in a good position after landing. She obviously saw a good stride into the fence, is riding forward and is already looking for the next jump.

Tidworth The gap between the first rail may have confused the horse, and he missed his stride completely. The horse slowed down and the rider just sat there hoping it would be all right. Better to have jumped the fence completely rather than try and fiddle a way through the middle.

Chapter 8

Ditches
Lucinda Prior-Palmer

What is your technique approaching a ditch and fence?

About 100 yards back, I just collect the whole boat together. If it's a straightforward fence like an open ditch and hedge or rail without any difference in the ground, I just sit up and keep riding and there probably won't be any difference in the pace. If it's a fence which is slightly hidden beneath a rise or fall in the ground, where a horse is suddenly going to come upon it, I have got to be going a lot slower with a lot more impulsion because the horse might spook when he sees the ditch.

Mark Phillips at Wramplingham A nice straightforward fence though a very deep ditch. You just come galloping along and take off anyhow. Everything is swinging but the horse doesn't look very happy. Perhaps he's bored!

Brigstock Horse thought this was very funny.

Somersault at Batsford Probably going too fast and the horse hit the fence above the knee. They say a fast fall is better than a slow one, and this certainly looks very nasty.

This "collecting the boat" as you call it, what actually do you do?

I definitely sit up. I go from a "Lester Piggott" racing position, so to speak, to an upright show jumping or dressage position. As I sit up I might give a yank on the reins because the horse is probably pulling quite hard by then.

Do you take several pulls or is it one long pull?

It will probably be several. Every horse is different but it will probably look like one long pull, sort of giving and taking in the middle. Some horses come straight back, others fight and fight and fight and fight, in which case you have got to be clever enough to do it early on so that he is not still fighting you as he comes into the fence. Otherwise he won't see the fence. Just by sitting up you will pull the horse back because your hands come up, but at the same time my rule is to do it early enough. You see so many people trying to get their horses balanced and back coming into a fence instead of well before a fence, so in effect they are stopping their horse at the fence. But whatever speed you decide to go at a fence, whether it's a slow canter, trot or gallop, you must be increasing in the last few strides. Not necessarily increasing your speed over the ground but just going into the fence with a forward design.

You are renowned for being pretty quick across country, but do you find that if you are sorting it all out a long way out, this slows you down?

Obviously the more checking and messing about you do, the slower you are going to be. But I think quite often it is not so much a reduction in m.p.h., as just a general gathering of the horse, re-balancing the horse. A horse in a three-day event is galloping on a long, flat, relaxed stride, otherwise he wouldn't be able to go the distance. He learns to gallop on a relaxed stride, so really you are not so much slowing yourself up as gathering the boat together by just sitting up and pulling one end and kicking the other. Half the time I don't notice that I am doing it very much. Other times I have a hard-mouthed horse or a lazy horse and you really are doing something.

Rushall This girl has got it absolutely right.

Winkfield The horse straddled and when they do that they go backwards instead of forwards, so you have to do the whole thing again. It is the sort of thing that can happen when you persuade a horse to go in at speed and his speed makes him take off, but in his mind he simply knows that he can't make it. Not very pretty.

So you've established the collection and you've got the right impulsion and speed, and you're coming into the fence, and we've established that you want to create this forward drive. What do you do next?

Ride, really. One just holds on to the front end but not so tightly that they throw their head in the air and don't look, but you don't let it increase because you restrain one end a bit. If you are coming to a big open ditch fence, you obviously want to increase your speed and accelerate, in which case you would probably be giving slightly with your hands. It's an urging, really, from every bit of you that clings to the saddle. It's only really about the last year and a half that I've actually learned to kick and that is why I spent a lot of my time taking my whip out to my horses because I never actually learnt to take my heels away and go whang. That is why if you ever watch any old films of Be Fair, apart from the fact that he always sank back in the last stride, I seem to be continuously belting him which was me who'd never learnt to use my heels. But really when you increase into a fence, you are urging with your bottom, your thighs, your knees, your calves, and everything you've got, and if the horse is beginning to come back at you or you are worried that he is not going into the fence in the right enthusiastic fashion, then the heels. Then if that is not enough, the stick.

They are going beautifully even though the horse is having a look down. He has got quite close.

Do you think that not enough people have learnt to ride with everything they've got?

I'll make a really catty remark and say not enough people ride with their heads! I am just as much of a sinner myself three-quarters of the time. It is true and one watches it time and time again. I doubt if it is stupidity so much as ignorance, and I think the only thing that can replace ignorance is experience. The amount of stupid approaches you see is unbelievable, and the approach is everything. People don't seem to realise how terribly quickly they get from A to B on a horse, and the plans they made on their feet are completely nullified because they are going three times as fast on a horse and it happens so quickly. I do agree with you that a lot of the time I don't think any of us do use enough "oomph", and resort to our sticks instead, and we could do it perfectly well with what we've got.

Let's imagine now that you are in the air. Does this particular kind of obstacle cause most horses to look, and by looking does it mean that you've got any problems in the air?

I remember once at Luhmühlen, on Village Gossip, going over a big ditch with a tree trunk across it, and he just sort of stopped in mid-air. It was quite unbelievable. He's a very spooky horse and he took off and he just completely dropped anchor, and I shot out of the saddle, directly above him, still in a riding position. In cases like this, when your horse realises it is a ditch and he is not confident and he's a spooky horse, it is absolutely awful what goes on. It is not a problem you can foresee and you can't do anything about it once you are in the air. I think it is sheer balance and jolly good fortune if you can stay on.

The only time you can do anything about it is on the approach where you need plenty of strength and impetus. But once you are jacked out of the saddle by a sudden movement of the horse, it's like a ricochet and you hope you land back again.

Do you consciously pick up a horse after a fence or do they do it by reflex action?

Half and half. Over a big fence when a horse has put a lot into the jump, I make a definite effort to congratulate him because I know how I'd feel if I'd had to jump it myself on my own legs! The pat picks them up in the most extraordinary way, and your enthusiasm and encouragement urges them on. I used to waste five strides on congratulating my horse and myself after every fence, and I wondered why I got so many time faults, but now I sit down and kick him after he lands so after a time he soon gets the idea and away he goes. After a really big fence, you have to

do a lot of regathering of reins to pick up his front end and drive up his back end, so that he doesn't fall on his nose.

If somebody came to you for advice about schooling a horse over ditches, and perhaps the horse had taken a dislike to them, what would you recommend she should do?

Take up hunting! The rider could be the problem, not the horse. Actually it is very difficult once a horse has taken a dislike to ditches or water because it is quite difficult to make them go. You must be intensely confident of your own ability to get the horse over anything, and you must start by going over every single roadside gutter and ditch you can find. Stay on that roadside till you get over it and never let the horse get away with anything. It must learn to respect you because if it is stopping over ditches, it will soon start stopping over something else. Don't for goodness sake go fast, because though the horse will jump, he won't have seen the ditch till he's in the air and it will give him a fright. School him slowly, trot or even walk up to the ditch and just stand there and kick him on and on until he goes. Make it small enough so he can jump it from a standstill and then it's repetition, repetition, repetition, till the two of you are exhausted. Kick him and beat him, anything you like, to get him over, but make sure it's a fair ditch and not a ruddy great thing. He must have the confidence to go over anything, even at a walk or trot and as soon as he can, canter over it. In an actual event, don't drop everything about six strides out and ride wildly at it in a panic, because he'll immediately sense something dangerous. You must keep him together in your hands with his head high so that he can't suddenly dive his head and shoot out sideways. Kick him and get him going strongly with a short stride.

Windsor Horse is not worried about the ditch and has given it bags of room. Rider is in good position.

Ickworth It's a horrible fence because you are landing on the face of a bank which stops all forward motion. Very uncomfortable. The horse has jumped very short, and I would think he pecked. Rider has done a good job to stay there.

Tommy Buck at Brigstock Some horses like Tommy Buck and my own Village Gossip are ultra intelligent and you can never sit still and trust them. You will always have to be behind them saying "DON'T YOU DARE!" It is not cowardice but sheer intelligence by the horse who is always questioning. Here Tommy Buck is on the spooks and my guess is that he had to be beaten to make him jump. He's looking down at the ditch and it's not the easy fluent jump it should have been.

Do you look for anything particular about ditches when walking the course?

I look for what I call "rider stoppers". So often ditches frighten the riders more than the horses, but if you can just go at them the horse will take you over. Often one thinks "Oh, it's a ditch!" and you get worried about nothing. Also you have got to think of every single alternative that the horse can take. In your mind you hope and expect him to do one thing but you are semi-prepared for four or five other things. Then, of course, a sixth thing happens that you haven't thought of and it all goes wrong.

Geoffrey Freeman at Stoneleigh Horse is jumping as high as he can because he thinks it must be terribly dangerous! A very happy man on top. (Editorial Comment: Reason for happiness was that this was only fifty yards from the finish!)

Rushall This is a beastly fence, and very, very big. She probably turned in too close which is why she couldn't get up enough steam. This fence always frightens the life out of me and I give it plenty of room.

Are there any particular ditches that you remember?

Fence Two at Kiev takes the biscuit for being quite the worst fence that I ever wish to come across. Its approach was at the bottom of a four-in-one hill, and you couldn't get up enough speed to clear it. A ditch will always slow a horse down more than a fence without a ditch and so you need to go faster. At this wretched fence at Kiev, you had four strides on the flat to get up a monumental amount of speed. The Russians were the only ones to do it well because they got to the crest of the hill that preceded it and went flat out down the hill and over the fence. None of us dared go down a four-in-one hill at that speed. Strong riders like Richard Meade got their horses going in four strides, and luckily I had Be Fair who did it for me. Even so I hit it really hard coming down but managed to stay on. There were 22 falls out of 46 people.

Were there any complaints to the course committee?

An enormous amount, because Princess Anne fell off and retired, and Janet Hodgson smashed her teeth in. Everybody took it as a lesson in how not to do course building and one hopes it never happens again. It was such a pity it was the second fence.

Angela Tucker on Mooncoin going like a bomb at Cirencester She's thundered down the hill and shot across the ditch. Lovely!

Steeplechase course at Crookham Forget about the ditch and ride as if it were just a lovely hedge, and the faster the better. It doesn't matter how hard you hit a brush fence, within reason, because you can scrape through it.

Dauntsey Park He's got that look. He's not happy looking ahead and he's definitely looking down over his forelegs. He is aware that he is jumping more than a telegraph pole but he is getting on with the job.

Chapter 9

Water

Bruce Davidson

How do you approach a water obstacle?

Talking about standard level—let's leave out international level at this stage—this means we are discussing what the English call novice horses and in America we call preliminary horses.

If there is only an entry involved, and the water is not too deep, and the footing is good, and there is no obstacle in the middle of the water, or on the exit, then you can enter on a canter; the splash and spray factor isn't too serious. But if you have a fence in the middle of the water and a jump out as well, then traditionally you should try and enter the water at a trot. You want to avoid galloping in because the spray becomes bad and very often the horse can't adjust.

So you don't want to be going too fast because of the spray?

You want to do the minimum speed and let the horse sort of lower himself into the water. I like to approach with a bouncing canter, making sure they are balanced and are not making ground with long aggressive strides.

What would be your upper body position as the horse is lowering himself into the water?

On any drop you want to encourage your horse, once he has left the ground, to land on his stride and not to land on his hind legs first. You want your seat really close so that you are sort of coiled in your legs, then if you feel the horse hit and start to peck you can sit up quickly and take hold of his head and hold him up. For the horse, jumping into water is a little bit like going down a staircase in the dark. You think you are on the bottom step but suddenly you find that the bottom step is eight inches closer to your foot than you thought, or a foot and a half further than you thought, and you take a step into space. That is what jumping into water is like for the horse and at the time they are not sure whether it is three inches deep or thirteen inches deep. They tend to land stiff-legged, not knowing exactly where the bottom is, and not knowing if the bottom is going to be heavy with muck or just gravel. Your body

position has to be one of good stability, and in a position to support your horse with both your hands and legs so that you are able to hold him up.

Can we take "good stability" a little further?

The one thing you don't want to be is pushed forward as you go into the water. You are likely to come off the shoulder if the horse buckles because of the water depth, and therefore can't pick up his knees, or if he goes into some mud and starts to peck, or if he stumbles. I think this is one case where the double bridge can be of assistance because your hands are on either side of his withers and you have the support of your reins to help hold your upper body in the correct position. This way you don't hit the horse's mouth and your body will automatically come forward into a good position.

What happens on impact?

It depends what is on the bottom. This new idea of a solid bottom filled in with sand and gravel, mostly gravel, is not so good because it tends to shift; it's not like landing on rocks. Sometimes there is a suction factor when the front feet don't come out and the hind legs get bogged down, and when they do come out they haven't got any shoes on! It helps if the horse is athletic because it is a little bit like landing on a trampoline. If you land stiff-legged you will be jolted sky-high, but if you land and give, you won't jar yourself too much.

Some people sit way back when they come down a drop before going into water. Isn't that difficult because the reins get longer and they will have to gather them up?

I've always been taught to ride as fluently forward as possible and not to sit back and "hail a taxi" as we say. I try to encourage a horse to stay in as even and flowing a forward pace as possible, and at no point to break his stride, or break his breathing, or discourage him from making an honest and bold effort at a fence. There are times, obviously, when you have to sit back and let your reins slip and then quickly gather them up again. As courses get bigger, then you

Trout Hatchery Looks like the entry was too fast. You have concussion and a splash factor, and if the horse came galloping in and took a bold, aggressive leap, he would be unable to make the next stride because of the depth of the water. Rider was in too much of a forward position and is already coming off the front of the saddle. Horses don't fall on landing, they fall the stride after landing.

Tidworth The horse stood back and jumped too strong, and they entered with too much speed. They came at it like a normal cross-country fence and did not adjust to the fact that the horse has a footing problem in the water. His hind end is too high and the front end is going to buckle. The water does not look very deep.

have a lot more demanding jobs, especially into water which is a popular place to put a jump, and very seldom do you have water on a level approach with just a vertical fence in.

The more you sit down, the more unpleasant it becomes for the horse. As horses get older and wiser, they can sense when the ground is "suspicious" or when they have to jump into space, and they are just not going to leap into unknown areas.

I can remember Irish Cap when he had his first proper jump into space. I was very worried because he was much too bold. He leapt way into space and I went up into the air holding the buckle, and came down hard on top of the saddle. Every time he comes to anything that looks like he's going into space, he puts himself right to the bottom and snaps his knees and almost goes in slow motion.

Does the water have any physical effect on the horse?

I don't think it is in any way a refreshing factor. I think it is an exhausting factor. Any change of footing, for example grass to sand and back to grass again, is very difficult for the horse and they find it hard to adjust.

You can relate it to running on a beach, and imagine yourself running along the ocean at knee depth. How far can you run? There is a terrific effort to pull your feet out of the water and make each stride, and I would be surprised if you could run like that for more than thirty seconds. It is very much the same for a horse, and they have the extra problem of not knowing how deep the water is going to be. If anyone thinks the water could be refreshing, I doubt if they would like to be hit by a bucket of water in the middle of a tennis match! It would soak your clothes and make it that much more unpleasant for the rest of the match.

How does the water affect you as a rider sitting in the saddle?

It's only bad if you fall. Otherwise, your reins are already covered with sweat, which is why most use rubber reins and rubber palm gloves, and your boots are also probably covered with sweat. In fact, that factor can help you stick a little bit closer. You see a lot of people before the cross-country wet their hands and the inside of their breeches, and take a bit of mud and sand and scrub the top of their saddle and the inside of their boots to rough them up a little.

Do you do that?

Only once. When I was at Munich, exhausted because Plain Sailing had pulled like a train on phases A, B and C, Jack took some

mud and sand and hit the inside of my boots and saddle, and I said "What the devil are you trying to do?" When I got up on him I thought "Wow. That stuff really works." I've never done it other than that one time but one sees the English do it a lot.

If you do have a fall, is it very greasy when you get on again?

Boy oh boy is it scarey! It's like sitting on a bar of soap, you just fly from side to side. Your clothes are soaked and everything is washing about, and it's hard just to get back on your horse. Your saddle, literally, becomes a bar of soap and the horse jumps a perfectly straightforward nice fence and you slide forward and bounce off the pommel. Then you slide back and hit the cantle, and I think am I ever going to find the middle of this thing. Then you come to another straightforward fence, and he goes to the left and he goes to the right and you grab your martingale. It's terrible. Unbelievable. Your legs are slippery, which makes it impossible for you to get close to the horse, and you can't help but laugh at yourself while you are flopping about for the rest of the course. At the same time you have got to get it done and you have got to stay on, and you've got to help your poor horse that has had a fall.

Is this what happened at Montreal?

I still don't know how we came down; I have spent nights trying to figure it out. He jumped in perfectly. His ears went up, his neck went out, he looked at the fence and he went to it. Maybe the footing had deteriorated or maybe he hit a hole; I have come up with every possible theory and I have received hundreds of letters and photos from people who were there but I don't know what went wrong. I am just thankful that Cappy wasn't hurt.

Were you hurt, because he was standing on your leg wasn't he?

He was standing right on my leg, so I was sitting on the bottom of the pond, and I had my nose just above water. Luckily I have a big nose because literally I thought I was going to drown. Cappy was standing on the reins so he couldn't move and it was really frantic. Finally, I just took my elbow and smashed him in the knee and he lifted his leg and I got out.

How do you start schooling a green horse?

That's the Number One Question. Water is a little bit unnatural but if you are going to compete at top level, he is going to have to negotiate water and there are many combinations into water. You can get fences in the middle, you get jumps out, you can have

Trout Hatchery 1 I know that fence pretty well and my guess is that he slipped on the approach. He was probably hesitant to enter the water in the first place. Maybe he was tired because it was late on the course, he got under it and he hit it on the upward motion.

Trout Hatchery 2 Nothing you can do but pick yourself up, get your horse up and hope that he can finish the course. There are six fences still left to jump.

Wramplingham When jumping out, enter the water cautiously so that the horse has a chance to evaluate the situation and see what is expected of him. The water is quite deep here, so once you are in and the horse sees the way to get out, you can let him have a couple of strides to negotiate the obstacle. Horse is jumping well and rider is well forward, helping the horse to bring his hind end up under him.

angles and you can have drops.

The way you first of all initiate a horse to water makes the difference. What we do is to find a stream that is very shallow and that has good footing, and we let the young horses go back and forth across it so they are familiar with getting their feet wet. They get to know that it is only two inches deep, it is not slippery and there's no suction. Then we take a set of show jumps down there and put them on the edge, and let them trot over a little jump, and plop into the water, and jump out again. We make it into a little game. Then we put another little jump on the other side so that you can have an "in and out" in the water, and they get used to looking at the fences and forgetting about the water. You can go on to build every sort of option that you can have in a competition.

Do you keep the fences very small?

Yes, and even with the old horses I do it in the spring before the season starts. We want the horses to get to the stage where they just don't consider the water. They have been through it so many times and it has always been shallow and they've never slipped or hit a stone, and it doesn't worry them.

We are lucky because we have got four or five streams on our farm, and in most of the major fields they have to cross water.

What happens when you get to an event and the water is eighteen inches deep and not two?

The horse doesn't know it's eighteen inches, and to him water isn't any consideration, it has always been two inches. By the time he is in the water and found it is eighteen inches, he is already in, so what's the big deal. Then you quickly take him home, put him right

Everingham With obstacles in the water, horse can have difficulty judging the height.

Chatsworth 1 Horse has shut his eyes because of the spray and splash factor, so if there was another obstacle coming up, he probably wouldn't see it in time. There is also a darkness and lightness factor here, and the water is deep.

I think you've got to get your horse familiar with all types of fence, not just water, rather than enter them in competitions and see how far they go. That doesn't make sense to me. You run the risk of getting yourself and your horse hurt, holding up other competitors who have really done their homework and maybe end up scaring what could be a really nice horse. It's better to spend more time and money training the horse over someone else's cross-country fences and paying whatever the fee is. You can take your time over the fences, walking and trotting if need be, so when you go in for your first competition, the horse has been introduced to many of the fences already.

Do you school your older horses at the beginning of the season?

I always give them two or three schools before the first competition, which doesn't mean galloping complete courses. The first time it means trotting between fences, and the second time jumping three or four together, followed then by a mile and a half course, so they will have been in the water three times. If they go well in the competition, and the water didn't present a problem, I just go from competition to competition and I don't bother to re-school them.

How about the young horses?

I make sure they go through water regularly at least four times a week. Sometimes just hacking through streams, or going through the mud hole. If the horse was in any way worried about water, I would give him a proper school the day before the competition and convince him that getting his

Chatsworth 2 Horse is jumping from water to water very well. It is never clear because of the thrashing and splashing in the water, exactly when the horse is going to get off the ground so the rider can get left behind. This rider is behind the motion and his body is not going with the horse.

back in his stream, and he says "Oh, it must have been my imagination".

You see kids at home schooling their horses through a deep pond just before an event, and the horses are scared to death even before they get to the competition. So the horses stop, not because of the depth, but because of their experience. If their experience is sound and trusting, then the one time they have to jump into deep water or run through a lot of water, they'll give it a go.

What do you do if you haven't got any water available?

You must find some water and take a couple of cavaletti with you. The other thing you can do is build your own big mud puddle, line it with some heavy plastic and put some gravel in. Keep it filled up with a garden hose.

feet wet isn't such a big deal.

If you've had a fall in water, especially with a young horse that is inexperienced, it is a much more serious fall than over a regular fence because water is artificial and slightly unnatural. If the horse goes down and gets properly submerged, then that is the frightening factor and then you come back to the problem that it's not the fence the horse is stopping at, but the water. I always like to have the feeling that when a horse enters a splash, he doesn't think about the water but only the obstacles. If the horse has a fall in the water and seems frightened, I would go back to schooling.

How do you get the horses used to water again?

We hack them down to the Brandywine, which is a very big river, and stand them up to their knees in cold running water. After they've been to the Brandywine a couple of times, they think it's really wonderful and it's like a whirlpool, almost a massage. They stand in the water for an hour and they go to sleep and nobody moves a foot. Sometimes I take a book and sit on one of the horses and read for a whole hour.

What have been some of the most difficult water fences that you've jumped?

The Trout Hatchery at Burghley was very difficult. It came late in the course, the vertical was big, it was really slippery and there was a sunlight/darkness factor.

To jump any vertical that size coming down a fairly steep hill is difficult, never mind the water. The water was black because of the shade, there was a lot of it, and there was a jump out. By that stage in the course the crowds were not too much of a factor because the horses were either used to them or were never going to get used to them. The slip factor, the vertical factor and the lightness/blackness factor made it the hardest splash I have ever done.

I think Munich was difficult. The water was very deep, well above the horse's knees, and it had a tremendous drop. Once in the water you had a ninety-degree turn, and then you had to jump a pretty good bank to get out. There was also a crowd factor because you had a ninety-degree turn to the left after you entered the water and the crowds were all in front of you.

The Dewpond at Wylye This looks pretty good and everything should be O.K.

Chapter 10

Combination Fences
Richard Meade

Let's say you are approaching a three-element fence on one of your international-class horses. What specifically do you do about one hundred yards out?

I first of all make sure I'm on the right line so that I know I'm going to arrive at the fence at the point I want to jump it. I might have a line on the three uprights of the fences or I might line up a point on one of the elements with a point in the distance. As I approach the fence, what I actually do depends on how well balanced the horse is. If he's going at a good speed and he's on the bit, and balanced, I'll do as little as possible as late as possible. Anything you do to slow the horse down is going to affect your cross-country time, so the later you leave it the better.

What do you do about fifteen yards out?

I make sure the horse is going at the right speed, which usually means slowing him down. What I aim to do is just to be able to close the hands and legs, and the horse comes back to me. That's what I'm aiming at. Very often you see riders struggling with their horses, but I think anything you do that can obviously be seen shows an unsophistication and is a long way from the ultimate.

Wramplingham This is a combination where you are offered a choice. You either go in and out separately or you take the parallel bar at the far end. Your decision depends on many factors but in a sense it is less effort and much faster to take the parallel bar. This decision has to be made when walking the course.

In a three-day event you're riding to get round with the minimum effort, so for a horse to jump twice requires extra effort. You would have to be sure that the approach was good but the parallel bar doesn't look too difficult and I would probably have chosen it, but I wouldn't mind the other route either.

How not to take the Combination at Brigstock. The horse has ridden in to the fence with no stride at all, got it completely wrong and hit it very hard. This shouldn't happen. The horse is taking off quite happily with his ears pricked and he's not expecting trouble, but he's right underneath it.

In cross-country, you must not be in front of the movement because if you hit something hard you're gone.

Does this subtle control require a lot of schooling?

It takes a very long time and with some horses I've never achieved it. Barbery, the first horse I rode internationally, was very headstrong and he took a tremendous hold, but if I moved my hands round on him or pulled at him, he went off the bit. Eventually, I got to the stage where I could close my hands and my legs and immediately feel his hind legs come up underneath him, and he would go into a collected gallop. It also happened with Laurieston, the horse I rode in Munich. The first time I got the feel of him was at Eridge during the final trial for the Olympics. He was a very headstrong horse and it was very difficult to keep him going straight because he would twist in the air. He would get too close to a fence and tuck his hind legs on to one side, and therefore one had to keep a very still hand on him and make sure he went absolutely straight. Cross-country epitomises the whole principle of riding, which is to keep the horse between the legs and the hand.

When you are riding cross-country, and in particular a combination fence, do you choose to sit in a safe position in case you accidentally touch something?

I very seldom get in an upright position where I'm sitting heavily in the saddle. I keep

107

Diana Thorne at "Which Way" rails, Burghley Diana was the only rider to go through this combination in this way. Everyone else took the parallel at the far side.

very close to the saddle and in those last few strides I might have my seat actually in the saddle but it's not a conscious thing. I think it's important to keep very close to the saddle, especially the thigh, because you're "there" if something goes wrong.

Having achieved this collection with the horse, do you push on firmly or do you let things take their course?

It depends whether you see a stride and realise you must make up lost ground or whether you can just hold quietly back. But if you do see a stride about four or five strides out, then you mustn't upset the equilibrium as you ride for it. Theoretically, you should ride in a balanced way forward if you want to gain a bit more ground.

Are you of the school of riders who likes to see a stride?

I think you owe it to the horse to try and ride a fence right and to that extent I like to see some sort of stride. It may not be noticeable to people watching because I'm not hooking them up, but you can adjust just like a jockey by either riding them forward a bit more or by holding them. But the more subtle it can be, the better. If you're dead wrong going into a fence, say you're going downhill at an upright gate, then no way do you just ride the horse into it and let him sort it out. You've got to have a horse trained to get himself out of trouble, but you owe it to him to come in balanced at the right speed so that he's got a good chance of jumping the fence without too much trouble.

Brigstock A very good example of the horse going forward. His hind legs came up well underneath him as he landed and he's able to do an extremely good jump over the second element. No time lost as far as the jump is concerned.

When you've landed safely over the first element at a combination fence, what do you consciously do to get over the second element?

You must keep the forward impulsion going and you aim to keep the horse on the bit, keeping a contact on his mouth and keep him going forward.

Is there anything particular that you must watch out for on combination fences?

You have this added dimension in eventing of uneven ground because if you have a steep slope it can make it very difficult to see a stride. Other things you get are "angled fences" and "corner fences". If you are going down a slope to a fence you must make sure the horse's hind legs are underneath him because if he's on his forehand, he can't pick up his shoulder so well or the front part of his body. If his hind legs are underneath him, that frees the front end. But in all combinations, whether they are sunken roads, Normandy banks or straight combinations on rough ground, it's all a question of balance and impulsion.

What advice on schooling would you give someone who had a horse that had done well at hunter trials and wanted to start eventing?

I would want him to reach the stage of training where he could control the horse's speed and impulsion coming into a fence, and dressage is theoretically designed to do this. If dressage doesn't do this, then it's the wrong sort of dressage. The whole thing

Badminton 1976 At every fence like this you want to approach fairly slowly with plenty of impulsion. A good bouncy canter is best so that as they get to the fence the horse can see what's going on. He's going to be looking at what's on the other side at the exact moment you're riding him forward, so you want nice impulsion and not to be going too fast. If you come in at a gallop, he'll say "Help! What's that?"

This rider is doing well. She's going forward and she's got good contact.

about eventing is to try and train the horse for all phases of the competition in a constant way. But when he first sees show jumping grids or cavaletti, he is bound to be confused, and especially if he sees three fences in a row with bounce strides.

This question of bounce strides, is it something the horse actually has to learn?

Yes, he does. He starts off with a grid only a foot high and this teaches him to land and take off again. It's a good gymnastic exercise and since it is not something that occurs in show jumping, it has to be schooled for specially. It's only in recent years that one's had bounce strides.

Do you think combination fences are getting harder and harder in international competition?

I think there's now a "flattening out" of the "difficulty curve" but personally I think combination fences are good for international competitions. They can be built so that horses aren't going to hurt themselves and yet you have to ride them right, and it's a good thing to have obstacles that require riding ability as opposed to sheer jumping ability on the part of the horse. Combination fences with difficult distances or angles can bring about run-outs and stops which don't do the horses any harm but do give the right influence to the cross country. There was a fence at Burghley, it wasn't a real combination, which had a rail halfway down a bank and the ground was very

uneven. There were four different ways to jump that fence and all four were used successfully, and the difficulty was not the fences but the approach over undulating ground. I think a fence that requires riders to go back and look again and again is a well-designed fence. The tenth fence at Montreal, the Gromont Slalom, required a lot of consideration because it was built on the side of a steep slope that required a turn through 180 degrees, jumping three fences. The night before the cross-country there were still riders looking at it after it got dark. It was not a tricky fence for the horse, rather was it a difficult test of riding.

Are there any fences that you remember as being particularly difficult?

The second fence at Kiev was one. You had to go round the side of a hill and there were only about four or five strides when you got to the bottom to straighten up and accelerate, and it required very strong and decisive riding. But I think the most difficult combination fence I've ever jumped was the 23rd fence at Munich. You came up a hill over a bank, turned left, and went down three strides towards a dip. You then had to take off over a two-and-a-half-foot fence with a six-foot spread up on to the platform of a Normandy bank. The platform was nearly three feet above the level from which you were taking off. Then 14 feet away on the far side of the platform was a three-foot-six upright, and the landing was on to a bank with a ditch between the bank and the fence.

The big question was whether the horse could put in one stride or two, and whether the fence should be jumped at an angle and how fast. Some people trotted it, some galloped it, some people went straight and some went at an angle. When I walked it, I could not see an ideal line and I simply couldn't predict how the fence would jump. I was the last to go for the team, on Laurieston, and I knew that all three of our riders had had refusals, one each. I thought the only thing to do was approach it at a slow canter with as much impulsion as possible so that the horse would land on the ledge and sort himself out. I didn't feel there was much I could do after that except keep the horse balanced, because if you pull the horse in the teeth, all you're going to do is upset the rhythm. I approached the fence at an angle to give me slightly more room and tried to ride it slowly with bags of impulsion and hoped the jumping ability of the horse would get me out the other end. You needed masses of impulsion because you have this problem of losing momentum when you are jumping uphill. That was by far the most difficult fence on the course and there seemed to be no way of jumping it. After we'd walked the course we went back to the training area, and some of the competitors had built a replica of the fence to see whether the horses would take one stride or two. I saw riders being invited to go and jump it and they were all putting in two strides. I didn't want to know anything about this because I did not think it was relevant, and anyway it was the ground that was important and you couldn't recreate that fence anywhere else.

How many strides did you get?

I got one stride, but once he was on the ledge, Laurieston was committed, and I just held and rode and kept my legs on him. He hit the fence coming off, but not very badly.

Wylye You've got to be absolutely certain of your line going into a three-element combination like this.

It's very easy for your horse to go off its line when you're jumping angled fences and there's no room to alter direction if you've only got one stride between the elements. You can't jump them on the turn.

Chapter 11

Roads and Tracks

Sarah Glyn

What sort of planning do you do before the roads and tracks section?

After a bit of experience you get into the swing of it, but I remember my first big event very well. I drove the roads and tracks twice, sitting in the front seat of the car so that I could see exactly what the terrain was like. I had a map, and a notebook, and a pen, and I made meticulous notes with a synopsis of each kilometre. Then I went home and worked out how much time I would spend on each kilometre, made allowances for hills where I had to walk, and grassy bits where I could canter. I wrote my notes down and pinned the paper to my arm so I could see it as I rode along. So the first event I did entirely by the book, checking my notes against the time all the way.

What do you do just after the start?

I've only really ridden three horses in three-day events. If I'm riding The Wheeler Dealer, I move off at a restricted collected canter, mainly because I can't stop him! As soon as possible, I try to settle him down and get into a rhythm. I try and get him into the pace that will suit him best without using too much of his energy, or mine for that matter.

When do you start to look at your watch?

I look at it very carefully before the start to see that it's correctly synchronised with the event clock. You must get it absolutely on the dot. I have an ordinary watch on one wrist and a stopwatch on the other, but I have to remember to wind them up beforehand! The watch has a beautiful clear face but I find on the steeplechase that it interferes with my wrist. Lucinda (Prior-Palmer) is very clever because she's got a watch she can tape to the back of her hand.

Do you carry maps or anything?

I carry absolutely everything! I have a piece of paper strapped to my arm with all my times, and then in case I fall off and get that covered in mud, I have a postcard in my pocket with more notes. I carry a map in case I get lost; I know it sounds ridiculous, but,

for example, you can get awfully lost on the flats of Holland, and it's foggy, and all the dykes look alike. Some kid might move a marker and you can get lost quite easily. I also carry glucose pills in case I get bored.

What do you think about?

Usually whether my horse has got the right attitude, and if he hasn't I'd better do some chatting to him. Luckily The Wheeler Dealer is a horse that wants to get to the other end as much as I do, but with another horse I rode you've got to say "Isn't this fun. Aren't we going to have a lovely time!" The horse thinks you're crazy but it's like talking to yourself in a way.

What happens if you catch somebody up?

I get frightfully worried because I think I must be wrong and perhaps I've made a mistake on my timing. Unless you're very, very self-assured, it could be you that's wrong whether I'm catching somebody up or they're catching me up. I don't really like to see other people as it breaks my concentration, though on some foreign events people are very friendly and wish you luck and so on. Sometimes you might see someone hobbling home because they've broken down on the steeplechase, and that's not a very cheerful sight.

What do you do at the end of Phase A when you are approaching the steeplechase section?

Somewhere on Phase A I like to give the horse a two-hundred-yard pipe opener to clear his tubes, because he's only walked, trotted and cantered so far. Depending on the terrain, I'd want to do that about two and a half to three kilometres before the end so that he's got time to recover before the start of the steeplechase. Then on the last kilometre I put my stirrups up a couple of holes to adjust them for the steeplechase riding. I like to arrive at the start about two minutes early in case there are any adjustments to be made. As you know, Phase A runs straight into Phase B, the steeplechase, so it is up to you to gain the extra time. I have someone to meet me at the start of the steeplechase with spare stirrups and so on, and also it's nice to hear how the steeplechase is riding and whether people are making it in the time. Also the horse might want his mouth sponging and the bandages might want checking. I always sew the bandages on myself beforehand so I've only myself to blame if they go wrong. I usually have bandages on the front and sometimes behind, but it often depends on whether you are going to jump into water and how far the water is from home. Bandages absorb water and that is more weight. So I like to have a helper in the box to check everything.

Chris Collins talks about the steeplechase section later in the book, so let us assume you have completed the course, safely, and you go past the finish breathless and exhausted. What happens next?

I let him run down gradually from steeplechase speed, through the canter, and degenerate into a trot. I keep him on the bit but try and keep my weight off his back. I then sustain the trot while I check whether he is lame or not. My friend and helper, the one I call "Wheeler's Wife", stands two hundred yards after the finish and she checks from behind to see if the horse has lost a shoe. If he has, she will get the farrier out and I'll try and get to the start of the cross-country in time for him to be shod.

If he wants to keep trotting I let him, but unless you have a wonder horse, he's going to want rest and he'll know when. He'll usually want to walk but I try to go as far as I can with the run-down before he settles for a walk.

I find horses tend to follow the same pattern. During Phase A they are all "oomph" and it's just a matter of getting them under-way without taking too much out of them and taking too much out of yourself, whereas Phase C is a matter of recovering from the steeplechase and giving them enough time to get themselves together again. It seems amazing but you've got to keep going to maintain four minutes a kilometre. As soon as you are lenient and think "Poor little darling, I'll let him walk", you have to pay for the time you let him relax. You then have to belt him in the ribs and get him going again.

Now you've already covered nearly ten kilometres, about four in Phase A and another five in the Steeplechase, and you've still got another ten kilometres to go in Phase C. At this point, are you essentially dealing with a horse that needs to be cheered up, or one that has regained his strength and needs to be controlled?

It depends on the horse, but in any case you must start playing off the kilometres to the horse's stride. You realise that you are going to have at least one very slow kilometre, and you'll have to make it up about half way through. Then the last few kilometres you will try to give him an easier time.

I think it's always a good idea to have two minutes in hand so that I can have a twelve-minute halt before the cross-country.

Can you remember any three-day events where the roads and tracks phase was particularly difficult?

I remember Windsor once being foul. The steeplechase was at Ascot Racecourse and you had to make it back through Windsor Great Park and a lot of it was along the side of a road. There was no verge and this caused problems because firstly you had to trot on the roads and secondly you've got studs on. So are you going to take the studs out and risk slipping on the steeplechase, or leave them in and risk slipping on the road? It's too much of a hassle to take them out between the phases.

Do you ever risk a short cut?

That's something you have to work out very carefully to make sure you are not missing a red or a white flag which are obligatory. But short cuts are very valuable because of the mileage you don't have to do.

Chapter 12

Uprights
Mike Plumb

Kilsby Horse is going much too fast and did not respect the vertical. Rider either didn't make the attempt to set the horse up, or couldn't, and she is paying for it.

Uprights, or verticals as you call them, are difficult for the horse and so many make mistakes at what appears to be a rather simple fence. Why is this?

Most verticals are "airy" looking and I don't think the horses respect them enough. I have spent a lot of time trying to analyse what their feelings are, and how they like to treat verticals. Verticals scare me because most horses want to run at them so I always try to help them a little bit; some I really take back and set them up carefully for the fence. I make up my time at another fence.

Would you show jump this type of fence?

I would on some horses. The ones that pull are apt to be a little sloppy. I would not worry on Better and Better because he is a very good jumper and respects all types of fences. He is not one that would rip my arms out of my shoulders to get to it. He is very much concerned with his own welfare, although he is brave at the same time, always a good combination. Lager I would definitely pull together as he is not so athletic and I would really make him pay attention.

What do you mean?

Let me give you an example. He had just taken a big brush fence with a ditch on the other side, and he was really going on a little bit. He was hard put to stop and he was going to take this vertical fence at the same gallop as he took the last one. All of a sudden I had to rip his teeth out and say "Come here now. I don't want you to run and jump at this fence because I don't trust you." Perhaps I should have let him do it his way, but I didn't trust him and I had other places where I could make up time, so I did it my way.

How about a trakehner where the ground drops away from a single rail. Would you ride at the base of it?

The type of horse I most enjoy riding to that type of fence is a horse that is totally game. So you come off the last fence and you are galloping and you get a smug feeling two or

Dauntsey Park Here is a snake-type fence over a ditch and horse is jumping very well and looks confident. Perhaps rider is a little bit forward and a little bit over the horse's front end, but basically a very good position.

Kinlet Whatever the rider has done, it has worked well because the horse is attentive, confident and looking where he's going. Not a straightforward vertical because the trellis is distracting and horse has quite rightly treated the fence with due respect. Rider is in perfect position.

Stokenchurch In a triple combination like this, you have to leave a lot to the horse to get it right. Horse and rider have a lot of trust with each other and though rider is a little bit loose with the reins, and a bit far from the saddle, nevertheless they are going well.

three strides away that the horse is with you. He is drawn to the fence and you know there are no short strides, but if there are he will adjust, and he wants to keep coming through and over the fence.

What if the horse is not so bold?

I would pull him together about ten strides away. I would give him a half halt and pull him together with my legs; make him come from behind with my legs so that he is in my hands and I have coiled the spring a little bit. Then I have the wherewithal to increase my stride when I like it or hold him down a little bit until I see the distance.

It doesn't always work out, but I find in most cases that I can see the distance and ask for the increasing stride when I want it, and really go to town with the heels to get them off the ground.

I think the danger is to run them off their feet from ten strides out and that is where they can spit the bit out. But the place to enforce their pace is from maybe two, three or even four strides out because that way you don't lose them when you get to the fence.

Do you do any adjusting after four strides out?

No. If you start to fiddle with them then you are going to confuse them, and maybe even scare them.

When you are driving him forward, are you using your spurs?

Yes, and of course they want to go away from the spur. I find it difficult to use my stick there because I am always afraid of a run-out. If you think you are in trouble preparing for such a fence, I would go after them with my stick from way out and make them run from the stick for a couple of strides. But you must always be able to get them back again because a runaway horse to the fence is a disaster. They can make a mistake by putting in a bad one and falling, or running out, or stopping. When they are running away it is very easy to lose them when they get to the fence.

If you can't trust a horse to carry you to a fence, it is a terrible feeling and it will make you very tired. If the horse has a problem and doesn't want to go, then you have to

Brigstock She is slightly behind her horse with loose reins, and she's not over her legs. I would not like to be in this position over a vertical because if the horse pecked you would be in trouble. Looks as if she's used her whip over the fence, but horse is jumping well.

straighten him out right at the beginning of the course.

How do you straighten him out?

If they are creeping underneath their fences, then you have to use the stick. I use the stick in front of the fence, and I use it on landing, but I don't like to use it over the fence because there is not much he can do in the air. They must know that when they make a mistake it is wrong. Some horses are afraid of your voice and I see no reason why you can't holler at them and sometimes they learn from that.

How would you approach the kind of vertical that is preceded by a ditch? Would you ride to the bottom of the ditch?

I try to get as close as I can, and I would be a little bit behind the motion in the beginning because I find it easier to ride a horse with my seat behind the motion. I would not be galloping on from too far out because when you approach the fence, there is no way you can go on increasing. You've done away with your spring action and he is not coiled

Builth Wells She either came too fast and got short to it, or came too slow and horse was too late with his front end. I think it's something that we are all frightened of. The horse is not about to get over and there is little the rider can do but hang on and hope to survive. Her position is as good as can be expected in the circumstances. When they come in too strong and a little bit out of control, they can easily make mistakes, and that's what always scares me about verticals.

If the rider hangs on and waits, there is always the chance the horse will get over somehow and save the sixty points!

125

any more, so there is really nothing left to deal with a difficult situation. It is much easier for a horse to deal with a bad distance if he is going forward with this coiled sort of action.

Does the ditch act as a ground line?

Yes, it does, but it is a difficult ground line and one that horses rarely look at. It doesn't set them up for the fence, it sets them back.

I happen to be going through a group of horses which are "lookers", and they are very careful about things like that, so I am very concerned with that type of fence right now. The ditch in front of a vertical makes a horse look. If you put a pole above the ditch, just laying it on the ground, I think that helps the situation.

Tweseldown Too much speed, with the horse really not paying enough attention. Rider is in a very precarious position and won't be able to help the horse very much on landing. Horse has not respected the vertical.

How about a vertical that was just a single pole?

I think the air is the thing that would make me want to throttle back a little more because they might get strung out and drop a leg if they were going too fast. I would want to make them bend and round up over the fence to encourage them not to be sloppy. With verticals I would always want to try and see where I'm going, where my spot was. It is not that I don't do that as a matter of course, but for that type of fence I want to have my horse in hand and know where my take-off is going to be. A spread fence that leans a little is a bit easier and you can let the horse handle it himself. I am inclined not to trust any horse at a vertical, in a competition.

How about schooling?

I would kind of let the reins go to see what he would do and I think that would tell me a lot about how he would behave in a competition. Let him figure it out for himself.

If you were starting to school a young horse, would you start with a ground line for the verticals?

Yes, I think so, but I have had very few horses that I have taken through novices, preliminary, intermediate and so on, because I've mainly ridden horses that have been given to me already trained. It is more fun starting them from the beginning but it is very rare in this country.

Jumping verticals is something we don't spend nearly enough time on. I think it is because it is not a very nice-looking fence, it is straight up and down, and if you don't put many rails in it is not a very encouraging fence for a horse to jump.

What about an upright that precedes a drop?

It depends on how much of a drop there is. If you have a horse that is a "looker" it pays to gather him ten strides away and from two or three strides really get into him and make him jump strong to it. If you get a horse that is a little chicken, you get them coming to it from three strides out and they'll jump it, maybe reluctantly, but as soon as they see the drop, they'll just lower themselves and perhaps hit it behind, but sneak over it. So you are not doing that much damage if you ride them a little bit stronger and see what they will do. But don't be too aggressive.

What about the rider who doesn't see his distance, because a great many riders don't have a very good eye?

I would make sure that the horse is in balance, though this is true with most any fence, and be certain that he is not running away, and that he is not on one rein if you have come on a turn. Then I would forget the eye and just ride for the fence.

Would you hold his head up a little bit?

I think we all make the mistake of putting a martingale on and having it too tight so when he puts his head up he is against it. He'll put his head up when he wants to see the fence; sometimes we put a running martingale on too tightly so when he puts his head up to look at the fence, it catches him and changes his concentration. You should avoid a running martingale if you can because horses need to look at their job and you may not know how to put it on properly or what adjustments should be made. If it's too tight, then you are jerking against the martingale instead of his head and you are not stopping him.

Speed and Galloping
Chris Collins

Did you get good at cross-country by listening to advice and comment or was it something you had a natural talent for and learned by yourself?

I came in on a different route from most people because I spent a lot of time racing long before I ever did eventing, and I started by regarding the cross-country as something very similar to steeplechase riding, which was in fact quite wrong. I now regard cross-country as a specialised form of riding all on its own.

Do you have a particular technique?

I think it's a compromise. You must go as fast as possible consistent with being safe and delivering a clear round, and you shouldn't take risks. I can't say that I have a particular technique because there are different ways of jumping different fences, but I have a number of principles I apply which have evolved partly from my racing background and partly from Lars Sederholm's instruction.

What are the considerations if you've got to cover about nine hundred metres of open ground between fences?

Firstly, you've got to analyse the ground because the terrain can be as important as the fences themselves. To take a simple example, it's more tiring for a horse to go uphill than down, so you would steady him, or make him go slower, or even make him a little bit angry to get him up the hill, and then let him free-wheel downhill. You must also consider what the going is like. In a major three-day event, the course is stringed off so there's not a very wide space, but quite often the line from one fence to the next can be up one side, not necessarily the middle. The first principle is to have a very close look at the terrain and make up your mind beforehand how you're going to ride that stretch, but this, of course, can vary, and you must be ready to change your plan later.

You may find the horse more tired than you thought, in which case you might have to wake him up, or he may be running freer and you have to settle him. You must have a

plan of how you are going to ride your horse, where you are going to push on, where you are going to steady him, where you're going to get a breather, and then ride the horse as you find him. Sometimes you sit on him quietly and just let him lollop along, and other times you have to breathe fire and smoke into him to get him going.

Do you find that your horses tend to be unpredictable over long three-day events?

The thing with horses is that you can't make a master plan and stick to it, because that doesn't work the whole time. It's quite likely they will be different in soft going or good going, and the question of hills is very important. Badminton is relatively flat and Burghley is hilly. You can probably afford to ride faster at the beginning of a flat course and eventually coast home on a horse that is tired, whereas on a hilly course you must keep more in reserve and analyse the hills very carefully.

Can we discuss roads and tracks for a moment? I can't see any discernible pattern emerging at the start of roads and tracks except just to get the time right. Is it really as simple as that?

Some people have a sheaf of figures taped or sewn on to their jersey, and they mark off every kilometre, analysing the time very carefully. My policy on the roads and tracks is to ride the horse as you find him, but try and get ahead of the game. I always start off a little bit faster to give myself more time at the end, so if there's a hilly bit I might walk up the hill, or take it slower, and then perhaps canter down the hill. I use the terrain to give the horse the easiest possible time but with the principle of getting ahead.

So you don't establish a fixed-rate trot up and down dale?

I think that is too rigid an approach ignoring the terrain. It's a complicated mathematical formula to equate an uphill kilometre to a downhill one, and the time value of each kilometre will be quite different. One can do a four-minute kilometre followed by a six-minute one, and it would be almost impossible to work it out properly. What I do is to look at my watch every kilometre and work out roughly whether or not I'm ahead of the game, and do a little sum to see how

it's going. I like to keep about two minutes in hand so that when I arrive at the start of the steeplechase I have time to make some adjustments if necessary.

Let's say you've arrived at the steeplechase. Do you find that your racing experience stands you in good stead?

Actually I find the steeplechase a difficult phase! It's not racing and it's not eventing, and I think it's a phase we're inclined to ignore. There's even a tendency to just start thinking about the steeplechase when you arrive, even at Badminton. I find it very important to ride the steeplechase on the watch because it's vital not to go too fast and take an unnecessary amount out of the horse. To avoid interfering with my start, I press my stop watch with five seconds to go and I look at it several times during the round. I always know where the half-way point is and ideally—if I had the opportunity—I would find out how long it took to get from between the last two fences to the finish, and use that as a final check.

A lot of people in eventing haven't got used to the idea that the first fence on the course is a steeplechase fence and probably a good six inches higher than anything they've been promised. Is that significant?

Wylye Rider's position is good and sympathetic. They are lolloping along and taking it easy. Horse might want to flex his neck more when increasing speed.

Funnily enough, event horses are asked to jump so many different and unusual fences that when they see a plain, straightforward, steeplechase fence that a race horse would want to attack and eat, they are slightly suspicious of it. It's sort of black and looks rather solid and there isn't anything behind, so they are inclined to be a little bit careful. They could easily, if left to their own devices, back off at the first fence and jump it too slowly and carefully, so what I do between the start and the first fence is get the horse really strongly on the bit. Perhaps if he wasn't going really forward I might even slap him down the shoulder and I would sit down at the fence and kick him strongly in. If necessary I might give him a quick hit on take-off and landing, which speeds him up through the air. It's very important to get the horse on the ball since most horses are going to spook a little bit at their first fence. They're going at a different pace and they don't know what's involved.

The important thing on the steeplechase is to get them very strongly in hand so they draw into the fence and if they are not drawing you must put the strength into them, either with a shake up with the hands, or with a couple of quick kicks, or with slaps down the shoulder.

Tidworth Looks a pretty hairy jump to me. The girl is sitting well except her hands are too far forward, and her body position is good except that the knees are a bit forward. Horse's high head carriage is probably due to holding his head going into the fence because he got too close. That's why he twisted over it.

Do you ride much shorter on the steeplechase?

I probably ride one hole shorter than the cross-country, but I don't ride a great deal shorter because those saddles are not designed for it. The real advantage of riding short is to hold a horse that is pulling, but by the time they've been round there twice, there are very few horses that do pull strongly, and I don't personally have a big problem holding horses. I like to get into a central balanced position on the steeplechase phase.

Generally speaking, do you think that event riders find it easy to get into a correct galloping position on the steeplechase section?

Because they tend to ride rather long, it might look a bit untidy because you can see their behinds bumping on the saddle, but nevertheless it isn't necessarily doing the horses any harm. The general style would be more going with the horse and letting him do it, rather than having him swing off you. I personally tend towards the racing position for the steeplechase.

If a horse is capable of producing an economical gallop, is there a way to achieve that technically and do a lot of people fail to get the best out of the steeplechase phase?

Learning to gallop properly applies to the cross-country as well as the steeplechase. If

Tidworth He's riding a bit long.

Bramham She's going slowly but then she's just come up the hill. Horse is on the bit and rider's legs are in a good position.

you watch a young horse trying to gallop in an event, he probably doesn't go straight but will weave all over the place. He can learn a lot from dressage, which involves them being on the bit and going truly in a straight line, but it might take two or three years to develop. It's difficult to advise people exactly how to school their horses to gallop properly because there are so many totally different ways of going about it.

There are race horse trainers who have their horses out for twenty minutes and do very well, and there are others who have them out for an hour and a half, and they both get the same result. I personally believe very much in getting the gallop right. When they canter round a field, I make them do it properly and I always have them on the bit and I hold the reins in a bridge sitting up. I also ride shorter to get them balanced and I adopt a semi-racing seat. Having the horse in the right balance on the flat or between fences sets him up properly and if you've got him in a good balance, you can trust him more and dare him more at the fences.

What do you do to collect the horse when you are approaching a fence?

It depends on the fence but basically I find the best way is to do as little as possible! Rather than have a wrestling match with the horse, I do the minimum, and hopefully I have the horse in balance. I probably raise my hands a little, press down my legs and possibly give him a nudge to get him on the ball and warn him that something's coming up. If he didn't respond enough, I might do it a bit more to get him back on his hocks, and then accept the way he wants to jump the fence. If he gets too close to the fence, I might save him a bit with my hands, but otherwise I act more as his adviser than master and let him attack the fence in his own way.

Are you good at seeing a stride?

Usually I see a stride but sometimes there's a false stride so I try to be flexible. One of the easiest ways to have a fall in eventing is to see what people call a "long one" and then the horse puts in another extra stride.

Let's say you've reached the end of the steeplechase section and you've got an exhausted horse. What do you do next?

The one thing I don't do is to pull up abruptly because that's not good for the horse's soundness. I gradually come down from a gallop to a canter which is better for his legs and gets you on to Phase C with a good start. If there's a nice bit of flat ground for half a kilometre or so, I might probably go on cantering. Unless the horse is exhausted, I would then continue trotting and let him get into his rhythm. Most people start by walking and make up the time later, but I prefer to get into the trot and give him a walk later on when we've covered five or six kilometres. I would rather get ahead of the game in roads and tracks in order to have a walk or a breather later on. If the horse has come off the steeplechase very tired, which could happen with a young horse or if the going was very bad, then I would walk. Sometimes a horse is lame for a hundred yards after the steeplechase with a sort of leg weariness, in which case I would also walk, but my basic rule would be to go into a sort of slogging trot and try and get ahead of the game.

During the roads and tracks, Phase C, do you get a good idea of the horse's fitness and how he will take the cross-country?

Sometimes you have a very tired horse in the roads and tracks but at a big event like Badminton, as soon as they get back to the park with the crowds and the loudspeakers, the adrenalin begins to flow again and they perk up. If you have a bad Phase C, then you might be in trouble on the cross-country, but

Badminton Horse looks tired and rider is trying to breathe a bit of fire into him. He's keeping him together rather well but should be more off the saddle.

Cirencester. Steeplechase Fence on the Advanced Championship Course Should be sitting further back because if the horse had pecked, she would probably have fallen off. She's going fast and I would say this is a rather bold way to tackle this drop fence.

once they've had their ten-minute break, they very often recover.

Talking about terrain generally, do you have any particular technique for going round corners or up and down hills?

The basic essential for going round a corner is to have the horse very well balanced so he is between hand and leg. If you've got to check for the corner, it's very important to do it before the corner and then accelerate round it, rather like a car. If you pull him round the corner, you'll get a bad ride and lose control afterwards. For going downhill, the rule to remember is that the horse is much better at going downhill than you are, and I've never seen a horse fall forward. Don't worry if you feel yourself sort of falling down it as you will get to the bottom okay. You may have difficulty with a sharp turn or a fence at the bottom, but concentrate on getting to the bottom first and let the horse sort out the fence when you arrive. He will probably jump it better than you think.

What about going uphill?

One wants to save the horse and keep him between hand and leg. If there's a fence at the top, don't let him sprawl too much, and approach the jump strongly with plenty of energy. Again, the horse finds it much easier

to jump at the top of the hills than you would think.

Any views about studs?

You definitely want studs in cross-country. I think it's rather like boots with nails on if you go climbing in Scotland!

Are there any events you've done where you were particularly conscious of the actual terrain? Are there any courses that you've come to love or hate?

In England, three-day events are held in these beautiful parks where the going between the jumps is relatively open. On the Continent you can get extremely tricky ways between the fences which calls for a different technique, and a very difficult one was at Kalmthout near Antwerp. The course was in a forest and quite often you came round a corner and there were only four or five strides before you had to jump a fence. One had to have the horse very well balanced and ride on round the corners much faster than one thought possible. I felt I had to get to know the course very well indeed, and walked it four times. The Polish riders bombed round the course very fast, but the English had difficulties with their big thoroughbred horses and they had to make a conscious adjustment of technique, since one's natural instinct is to slow up at a bend where you can't see round.

Which is your favourite three-day event course?

The absolute supreme place, the capital of world eventing, must be Badminton, which is superbly constructed and in a lovely setting. I personally have never been lucky at Badminton as something has always gone wrong. I've either had a silly refusal, or expensively knocked down a show jump, or the horse has blown up in the dressage, but I think one has to recognise it as the premier cross-country course in the world.

Osberton For me, that's too forward a seat. I would rather see a straighter leg that's not heading quite so far forward, and the behind a little more down towards the saddle. Looks as if she's had a cut at the fence, given him a kick on take-off and gone through the air with him.

Dressage
Karl Schultz

Do you have a fixed routine with your horses before the dressage section of a three-day event?

All horses are different but I have a routine with Madrigal that I've found is very successful and I use a similar routine with all my horses.

About four hours before the time I am due to go into the dressage arena, I will lunge him for about half an hour, and the purpose of this is twofold. Firstly, I want to loosen him up, and secondly, I want to make him bored. After the lungeing, I let him rest for a while and then I take him out and do some dressage practice. This will probably take another half an hour, and after that I will rest him again.

Are the timings important?

These timings are approximate and you vary them according to your experience and what you know is good for the horse.

When he has a rest after the dressage practice, I take him out again and hack him round the fields or tracks wherever we happen to be, and after hacking I let him rest again.

And now the final bit of the routine is terribly important and it is something that more and more riders are doing, and I think really they have copied me.

Let's say it's getting fairly close to when you are due to do the test. What do you do now?

Exactly half an hour before the test, I take the horse down to the waiting area, outside the arena, and I let him stand. Sometimes he even falls asleep. Then when I am called to do the test, I mount him and immediately take him into the arena to do the test.

Don't his muscles get stiff and creaky while he is waiting?

I usually keep him warm with a blanket. But the whole object of this routine is to make the horse bored. He is not tired but bored.

You will see a lot of horses being ridden for two hours before their dressage test, but you will find these horses are not being worked. There is an important difference between working and riding.

Karl (commenting on himself) Horse is doing the extended trot and moving actively forward. The rider is good on the horse with deep knee and deep heel. Horse is going forward away from his leg but he is not on the forehand.

Let's go back to the routine and build up before the dressage test in an actual event. Tell me again why you have this cold start.

It is very difficult to explain because I have perfected this routine over many year's experience. But I found that if I rode a horse like Madrigal even ten minutes before the test, he just wouldn't go properly and there would be an explosion. That is why I developed this routine to get the horse bored without tiring him out.

Is there a difference between dressage training in Germany and in England and other countries?

In England there is a much greater emphasis on hunting in the winter, whereas in Germany we concentrate on dressage. On the whole I think the English and Irish horses are much better than German horses, and many more of the English horses are thoroughbreds. What I think is the real difference between the two attitudes is that

He is well on the bit and his hind legs are well underneath him. The horse is coming up underneath the rider.

Diagonally the legs should be the same. If the fore leg is that high, then the hind leg should be the same.

138

the English riders are lazy. They enjoy riding and hunting, and are very good at it, but when it comes to dressage they find it boring. And after all, dressage is very hard work, and not nearly so exciting to the average rider as hunting. You must also remember that in England there are plenty of opportunities for hunting and riding over countryside which just aren't available in Germany.

How long can you practise dressage at any one time?

Well, I think there is a good illustration of the difference in training between England and Germany. One of the German dressage trainers came to England to teach event riders some dressage, I believe Lucinda Prior-Palmer was one of them, and he found the average practice session was about three quarters of an hour. The German trainer was horrified. He made them practise for two hours at a time, and some of the riders found it very tiring.

The hind leg should be more in front.

Rider is too much in front and he tends to sit forward. He does not use his legs enough. Nice type of event horse.

139

That is correct. Rider is sitting very well.

Do you need to be very strong to do good dressage?

You need strength and energy to produce correct dressage and many riders are too lazy to build up the strength that they possess naturally. They like to ride but they don't like to work.

Is there any particular difference between pure dressage and event dressage?

In pure dressage, the horse holds his head much higher, he is more elevated, and his back is much stiffer. You have much more in your hands. The event horse is much more supple and I always say that he should be like rubber from head to toe. Event dressage is not nearly so difficult, but even so my horses can do flying changes every two strides and they can do a half-pass in canter which is much more advanced than is necessary in three-day event dressage.

Do you have more dressage trainers in Germany than in England?

I think so and also we have access to the military dressage trainers who are very good. So if you have any particular dressage problems, you can always get lessons from the experts. Also I think we are determined to get it right if we should have a problem with a particular horse. For example, when this German dressage trainer was in England, one of the riders said he couldn't get his horse to do a half-pass to the left. This trainer couldn't believe it. If the horse is capable of doing it, then you must keep practising until you achieve it. Sometimes the horse might have muscle trouble or be a bit stiff, but otherwise there can be no excuse for not teaching a horse something like a half-pass. It might be difficult and it might take time, but it should always be possible.

When do you start training your horses to do dressage?

Munich 1972 Karl Schultz at the canter on Pisco.

141

In Germany, we start them quite young, sometimes as soon as they are broken. We think that they must have learned some dressage when they are three or four, otherwise it could be too late.

How do you start them off?

We always start with a lunge, and the head is held in the right position with a piece of harness called a chamborn. A chamborn is different from a martingale in that it goes over the horse's ears so that the head is tied down in the correct position. I then lunge them over trotting poles which teaches them to pick up their feet. I find this develops the back and neck muscles and gives the horse that deep head position. Even when I bring one of my top horses, like Madrigal, up from grass, I will go through the lungeing work for about two to three weeks to get the muscles working because you can't just ride a horse straight away. If the back muscles are too weak, then you create stiffness, and the horse won't go on the bit or turn properly.

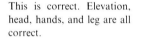

This is correct. Elevation, head, hands, and leg are all correct.

This is really good.

You can't train all horses exactly the same because they are all different. Some have more blood than others, and some are more hot-headed than others.

What do you do after lungeing?

You start by teaching him the natural paces—walk, trot and canter. For this you use a long rein so that you have no pressure on the horse's mouth. This means that the horse is only slightly on the bit and that you require only very slight movements of the reins to get the horse to turn left or right. However, if the horse is inclined to throw its head up, it will be restrained by the draw reins and after a while it will learn not to throw its head up at all. From there you progress to more and more advanced movements, and I think it is essential to use a good trainer in order to get it right. Horse and rider must work together as much as possible, but only a good trainer can really help you do it correctly.

Head carriage is too high.

Rider is just sitting there holding his hands low but the horse is not moving from rider's legs. Not good.

143

Chapter 15

Show Jumping
Celia Ross-Taylor

What's the difference between show jumping in eventing and pure show jumping?

The show jumping part of the three-day event is not to prove that the horse can do show jumping, but rather that it's actually capable of doing it on the last day. The horse has got to be able to jump and to use itself correctly; it's got to be athletic, to be able to work things out for itself and to think for itself. It can't do that if it's in a fuss and tearing about the place.

The rider has to be very accurate in show jumping, which the average event riders probably aren't because they don't have to be. In eventing, the horse must have a lot of initiative for cross-country, but in show jumping he must also be very obedient and the rider must have a very good eye.

Bramham Probably came all wrong at the fence, too fast, and the horse couldn't decide whether to take off or not. Horse has tried to jump a bit. Pretty comprehensive spill.

Burghley Very good contact and rider's hands are in line with the horse's mouth. Horse is a little bit flat over the top of the fence and he may have stood off a bit far. Rider's heel could be lower and her head up but that is not so important. What matters is the contact.

How big are the fences?

They are about show jumping size Grades B and C. They're not big but they can't be skipped over. A clever horse will get his rider out of trouble over them whereas if you meet a big Grade A fence and you're not right, the horse can't get over. In event jumping, a lot of horses sort of find a fifth leg and are capable of getting over, but with Grade A show jumping it has to be an incredible horse that can arrive wrong and still get over.

Do you teach your horses to jump correctly or do you do a lot of hunting?

If you've got a rather lethargic, timid sort of horse, hunting is probably very good. I personally prefer show jumping and I start all my horses off on show jumping lines. I have seldom hunted a horse that I've competed with. I like a horse that's pretty forward going and active by nature, and hunting is inclined to make them pull and hot up a bit. You're always having to pull back at them to avoid running into somebody's hindquarters and it's not doing their training any good. They must be trained to jump correctly in the first place.

What do you do to get it right?

A horse for steeplechasing or cross-country goes on a much longer stride and stands a bit further off its fences, whereas for show jumping you'd have the horse on a short stride, and you train him to do that with the help of acrobatic exercises. I put a pole approximately two and a half yards in front of the jump to make the horse come in close so it has to use its forehand. The horse trots or canters over the pole and then over the fence, taking off close to the fence. This way he has to bend his back. There are lots of schooling exercises like little short grids and bounces, but I use poles most.

What advice would you give to a friend who had a horse that went reasonably well across country but had problems with the show jumping phase?

If its attitude towards jumping was wrong, if it rushed at the fence with its head in the air and stood off in a long flat jump, then I would advise the trotting poles and patience! I also find jumping with a lunge is very good, again over the poles and the fence. A lunge with no contraptions, just a

Fenton Fairly typical style for event show jumping as horse has not rounded its back. Rider is holding on too tightly to its head, but they should jump this little fence without any bother. Rider looks anxious but horse looks very cheerful!

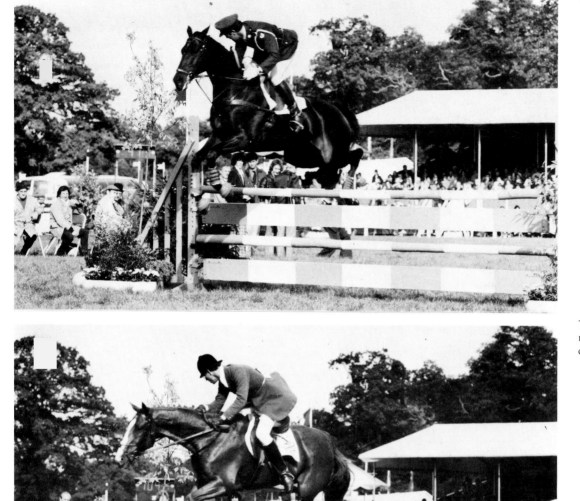

Horse got under the fence but has recovered cleverly.

They've come too close but rider is giving the horse freedom to get out of trouble.

Rider is in very nice position with light contact.

Probably fighting as he came in and put in a very bad jump.

Looks rather sprawly! He is in balance although he hardly appears to have jumped at all.

Horse is jumping with his head in the air. Horse might be afraid of being caught in the mouth or it might be incorrect training.

cavesson, so the horse is completely free, and it soon learns to work things out much better for itself. It has to, because there is no help or hindrance from a rider.

How do you deal with stiffness and tiredness after the second day?

I know it happens but I've never had a horse really tired and stiff. If they are good jumpers, the right type of horse, and they're properly fit, then there shouldn't be too many nasty moments. If they are stiff, then it takes a long time to ride them in and you should walk them for half an hour before schooling them on the flat. You must be prepared to ride them stronger because they might have got too strong from galloping or they might have got lazy because they're tired. You have to be prepared to alter your riding accordingly.

Have you ever been in the ring and realised the horse just wasn't going to go?

It did happen once in a three-day event. As I jumped the first fence, I realised he wasn't jumping at all, just not at all, and he knocked

Llanfechain It's such a small fence that they haven't bothered very much. Too much body movement, her lower leg is a bit far back and the contact is not right. Event riders tend to have their hands near the top of the neck for almost every fence, and this rider is holding hers in an odd fashion.

it down. Then it became a real problem, not just to jump properly but to get him over somehow. I had to catch hold of him, get hold of his head, give him a few nudges in the ribs to get him active and thinking and to wake himself up. If the horse really is stiff, then you should limber him up beforehand with lots of very small fences only about two feet six inches high.

Some horses are just a bit careless about show jumping. It always amazes me how they can survive and stand up to cross-country if they're really bad show jumpers. Sometimes they get to know what is a solid fence and what isn't, but in my own experience I find most horses hate to hit any fence. It hurts!

How do event courses at international level compare to an ordinary show jumping course at B or C level?

They are very much the same. I've always found good, true distances and they don't want to trap a horse. They should be straightforward courses with nothing too difficult about them. The courses are well built by people who also build show jumping courses.

Do you think that even at the top level, there is a lack of appreciation of the extent to which training for show jumping can improve the all-round performance of the horse?

Only a few people seem to appreciate the amount of schooling and dressage that is required, and it can take a long time. Perhaps it's more a question of patience than hard work. But the biggest problem event riders have in the show jumping section is simply to get the horse to bend its back, and that has to be done with the correct training. Most of the top event riders have their horses going very well and do well in show jumping up to B and C level. It is more the novice riders who have trouble with their show jumping.

Hollow back because of incorrect take-off.

Good cornering. Sometimes the corner can be more important than the fences.

Wellesbourne You can see they are in harmony. The horse looks happy and she's following very nicely with her hands.

Rider is jumping out of the saddle. It hinders rather than helps because rider has to come down with a bang which can't be pleasant for the horse.

Nicely together and professional, and a good relaxed landing position.

151

Chapter 16

The Team in Action
Lt. Col. Bill Lithgow

Is it very hard to pick the team?

We pick a short list for a start, and you take that effectively off the top of Badminton but not in the strict order that they finish. 1976 was exceptional in that the Olympics came earlier in the year than normal, and we therefore asked Princess Anne and Lucinda Prior-Palmer not to run their horses because we felt they were getting a bit senior and you can't go on asking the main question too often. But otherwise if you want to run about six horses, you'll pick a short list of twelve. You're tremendously dependent on soundness, of course.

Do you find it nearly always sorts itself out very rapidly in terms of selection?

Frank Weldon always used to say, and he's a very wise man, that you'll finish up by taking the half dozen sound horses you've got, if you've got them! When we went to Mexico in '68, we took with us four Olympic-class sound horses and two horses as spares, the only ones we could find in fact. Basically the horses selected themselves.

This year (1977), for example, we've got three that actually select themselves and underneath it we've got to put No. 4. For the fourth place, we've got about six, all of whom could go brilliantly, or all of whom could have a disaster, and so the selection of that one will be difficult.

Having selected your team, what do you do next?

One first has to make the administrative arrangements. We have always had a concentration period at Ribblesdale Park, near Windsor Great Park, where we have the use of Ascot Racecourse. This year, for one reason and another, we had the first concentration of a week rather earlier and a second just before the competition both at Wylye. I make the arrangements for the team to compete at the horse trials dressage at the International Horse Show. Then we have what I call a viewing day to check up on their general state of fitness; this is a bit expensive but you get them all at one place and you can compare them and it gives the riders something to aim for.

Then we have a competition in which they take part, which last year was at Osberton and this year it's at Locko Park. Throughout the summer, you're sort of in touch with them arranging this and that, clothing, rugs, that sort of thing.

The first time you actually live with them, so to speak, is when we go into the one-week concentration period, and the Chef d'Equipe makes all the arrangements for that. Each member of the team has his or her private trainer, though a few years ago we had a team trainer which made things a lot easier for me, but the riders didn't like it. They like to keep their own trainers and though we all get on fine, it's a bit of a minefield to operate in because we don't absolutely control their training.

Do you have any views on this personal trainer versus team trainer? The Americans go with a team trainer, don't they?

If you had a team trainer, who would it be? You won't find anyone in the country. There are a number who are capable of doing it, but there isn't one the riders would accept unanimously. They are all mainly riding their own horses and paying for them, so you can't impose a team trainer on them. Yet we've won a gold medal in Mexico with a team trainer, and we won one in Munich without. However, I don't think it suits our particular sort of temperament and geographically it's difficult. Some of them go to trainers because they live somewhere near them throughout the year. If, for example, you lived in Northumberland and you wanted Bertie Hill, it's a hell of a long way to go. However, I think the pendulum may swing in America too and they will revert to individual trainers. I don't think there is any set answer to the team trainer versus individual trainer, as it's so much a question of personality.

Going back to the schedule, how long is the concentration period?

In the early days, before the 1952 Olympics at Helsinki, the whole team went to Tony Collings for six months! But they were all soldiers so Her Majesty just went on paying

Lucinda Prior-Palmer on Be Fair

them, but you couldn't do that now. A few years ago, we altered the system so we had a week or ten days, because you don't need them for any great length of time. They're away from home with either one or two horses, and unless there's some very positive team training taking place, they soon get bored and fed up.

How about the final trial at Osberton or Locko Park?

There would be a week's rest after the final trial before the concentration period. But for a really big event, like the recent Olympics in Montreal, it gets slightly more complicated because you also join up with the dressage team and the show jumpers. Our aeroplane left from Luton and we wanted to arrive the other end about midday because there's a lot of settling in to be done.

Do you all travel on the same plane and sort of lead your horses up the gangway?

For Montreal, most of the riders went on scheduled flights with runners and swimmers and people like that. The horses are now loaded onto special pallets which are very strong, with two horses to a pallet, and these are loaded on and off the plane with a lifting platform. We normally keep them hungry the night before and the grooms carry lumps of sugar and carrots in their pockets to distract them when the plane is taking off. Once they are in the air, they get a feed and hay nets. On the whole an aeroplane is much more comfortable for them than a horse box travelling by road. Depending on the time change and the flight, we aim to arrive at our destination about tea time, so I seem to remember we left Luton about two in the morning.

Does it always run smoothly?

The arrangements for Montreal were absolutely first-class, and we were helped the other end because there were no quarantine complications. The only time it didn't really work was my first trip, when we went to Moscow. They had never run an event before, and there was nobody there to meet us. We arrived at about 8 o'clock that night, and it was pouring with rain and pitch dark; all they'd sent along to meet us were six three-ton lorries with no covers and no ramps, so I suppose they meant us to jump the horses in or something! What we did in the end was to take the ramp off the aeroplane, split it into two and make our own ramp. Coming back, we noticed a proper earth ramp about four hundred yards away on the edge of the airfield which was specially there for horses, but no-one knew about it and you couldn't see it at night.

H.R.H. The Princess Anne on Goodwill

Now that you've arrived at the event and with luck all your administration is working properly, what are your main problems? Are you starting to have to deal with the nerves of the individuals?

I've got to keep saying to myself "Cool it, cool it" and keep a level of control, because there is an awful lot to do and one is very inclined to get all tensed up. The whole aim and object, particularly with grooms, is to try and take the steam out of the situation. We all get excited from time to time and I say to the grooms: "Even if your rider drives you absolutely clean up the wall, don't kick him in the teeth till after the event". I always quote Mr Jorrocks' "Count twenty before hollering!"

Do you find it important to establish very tight time schedules?

We do virtually take charge of what goes on in the stable. We don't set out to alter the feeding in any way, but the vet, Peter Scott Dunn, might well discuss certain aspects of the feeding with the owner but basically they know their own horses best. We make all the arrangements for forage.

We have a regular routine to start each day. Peter Scott Dunn and I always "trot up" the horses at 7 o'clock with the grooms but not the riders unless they themselves mind. Everything is quiet then, and we get the horses straight out of their boxes, cold, and trot them up. This way you have got the same standard to compare them by each day. Then Paddy Morgan, the farrier, makes some coffee and if all is well we can relax for a bit. We don't insist on the riders being there but, of course, they are more than welcome. Sometimes at the event itself you have to watch them because it has been known for someone who is doubtful about his horse to go down at 5.30 and warm it up, but that is the politics—and the fun—of the game!!

Very often, the work they do hinges on the availability of suitable facilities. In Montreal last year, the dressage arenas were allocated at certain times; but, by a mixture of negotiation and pushing and shoving and bargaining, you could always get the extra arenas you wanted, and this was very much my job.

This is a rather personal question, but do you see yourself as a sort of all-purpose, friendly face to encourage the team?

I see myself as a face they've got to look at and I hope I can make it friendly! I wish them luck and do everything I can to help and that is the vital part of my job. I always go up to them immediately afterwards and say "Well done" and I think that is very important.

What sort of intelligence network do you set up? Do you do it by runners, or land lines, or radios?

Entirely by runners. We don't use radio links because, and this sounds terribly pompous, we don't think it's right. The next thing is they'll have a radio attached to the rider. In Munich we had six unisex bicycles lent to us by Raleighs and we used them on the cross-country day and it was great. Each nation has a team vehicle but you cannot use it on the cross-country course.

In Montreal, a message was sent back that a certain fence was a bit wet and was causing trouble, but it didn't get back in time to warn Princess Anne, and she fell there. I don't think, in fact, it would have made any difference, but there it was. I then went down to look at the fence and it took me quite a long time to get there. I am game for using anything, provided every other team has the same opportunity. You have to be very careful not to use privileged vehicles even by mistake; we had an unfortunate occurrence in Munich when one of our helpers hitched a lift in a VIP's Landrover round the cross-country course, not realising, in his enthusiasm, that as a result we could not thereafter use his information.

What sort of quality of comment do you get?

First class.

I normally have a filtering system and I ask someone like Lord Hugh Russell to organise the runners and pass the information to me.

I am then the one who passes it on to the riders. Now, no way am I going to tell an experienced rider how to jump a fence, but what I do want to make sure is that they have thought of every alternative. After the walk round, which they do individually because they don't like a team walk round, I get them all together and we discuss what the various alternatives are. There are probably only seven or eight fences that are anything to worry about, but we examine these in detail and we do this with the profiles of the fences. I insist that everybody has an alternative in case horses are slipping or something, or the way they want to go isn't working. But I find the riders are very helpful to each other and it is very interesting just to hear them talk.

Can you remember any really difficult moments when you had to direct or advise the riders?

I remember well in Munich, which was a very harassing afternoon and extremely hot, and everything was not going right. Mary Gordon-Watson had had a refusal, Bridget Parker had had a refusal and lost her way on the steeplechase course, and Mark Phillips

Richard Meade on Jacob Jones

157

had had two crippling falls. Richard Meade was the last to go and he's one of those people who reacts well to a crisis—the worse the crisis the more the adrenalin flows—and he came into the box as if he was just arriving at the annual church fête, and he said to me "Are we still attacking?" and I said "Indeed we are!". He went like a bomb and we were lucky enough to win. There are moments like that when you can help the team.

I have always hated any sense of trying to play safe. In Montreal, I felt from the word go that since we had had the good fortune to win the two previous Olympics at Munich and Mexico, no way were we going to play safe, but have a bloody good go at winning. But there was one fence at Montreal that the team were worried about, Fence 10 I think it was, and at the briefing I was asked specifically "Do you want us to take a chance at Fence 10?" I remember the actual phrase I used to reply was "No. I want to see you through it." I said that, on the grounds that over a five-mile course there were other places you can make up speed. Your basic approach is you're going for maximum bonus but you don't have to attack all the time.

What else happened to you at Montreal?

Dressage-wise, the thing I was worried about was all those flowers around the arena. Marvellous really, it was beautifully done, with those great slopes all round with masses of people in summery dresses. What particularly alarmed me were the little flower pots with pampas grass in them that were placed on top of the markers about two inches from the horse's nose. I lodged a complaint and we got them moved, but instead of moving them right away, they put them round behind the markers so they were still there.

Eventually Dick Stillwell and I got up and moved them ourselves, and it's interesting that in spite of all the massive security, no one questioned us for the whole three quarters of an hour that we spent moving the damn things.

What do you think of our chances in Moscow for 1980?

One thing you have to realise is the margin between triumph and disaster is terribly, terribly narrow. In Montreal, things nearly went wrong for the Americans but finally went right. We could so easily have beaten them but I don't think we deserved to; they were better. In Mexico we had three enormous slices of good luck, and you can't do without it!

The shortage, to my mind, is not so much of horses as Olympic-class riders; but people keep coming up. I am full of optimism and shall be desperately disappointed if we don't do it, but I couldn't actually at this moment tell you which horses are going to run. If we play our cards right, and have a bit of reasonable luck, we can do it and there is a lot of talent about.

Michael Moffat on Demerara

Chapter 17

Putting the Mastery to the test
Jane Pontifex

By now the reader will have gathered that there is one part of the three-day event which looms larger than the other two: one which particularly grips the Masters' imagination and calls for their greatest skill and attention.

Those who have attended a three-day event will know that this is indeed the case and that it is the second day, when the speed and endurance test takes place, which is the day of reckoning.

The tests on the other two days, dressage and show jumping, though essential parts of the competition, are important mainly as exercises in the training and technique which arm a horse and rider for their assault on the speed and endurance test, and this is reflected in the rules. A moderate dressage score or careless show jumping round can make only a dent in the advantage gained by a good cross-country performance, and many a competitor has risen 20 or 30 places on the second day.

The three-day event is not a specialized art form but a comprehensive test of the whole range of equestrian skills; the Master of eventing is no prima donna but a resourceful all-rounder, excelling in them all. He and his horse must, between them, display qualities of high courage, peak physical fitness, stamina, speed and athleticism, calculation and decision tempered by flexibility, a cool head, the ability to concentrate on each of the very different aspects of the competition in turn and, finally, great mutual trust and understanding.

In common with most other competitive horsemen, three-day event riders display a becoming modesty in their own achievements, giving most of the credit to their horses, but they do themselves less than justice. Even at a big international championship, there is little personal rivalry between the competitors: they see it as a pitting of wits against the course rather than against the other riders.

Senior technical adviser, Bill Thomson has been with the British Horse Society more than 25 years, travelling all over the country to advise on site-selection, course-planning and construction of fences—which, more often than not, means doing it himself, to his own high standards of craftsmanship, which have been emulated all over the Eventing world. His courses at Windsor, Harewood and Burghley have included two World and five European Championships.

If a long journey is involved, competitors will arrive on the scene of the competition several days in advance, to give their horses a chance to recover and acclimatize and to settle down to work again in their new surroundings. Riders must then focus their full attention on the five days involved in the event itself.

First is briefing day, when competitors receive all the necessary information from the organizer and are shown the course—driving round the roads and tracks, walking the steeplechase and cross-country. They will revisit the cross-country course several times before they actually ride it. Declarations close after the veterinary inspection of horses that evening.

Dressage normally takes up two days, the first two runners in each team riding their test on the first day, the third and fourth runners on the second. A panel of three judges marks each movement of the prescribed test and these marks are turned into a penalty score, to match the rest of the competition, so that the lowest is best.

The dressage test is to show the standard of training and competence of horse and rider. Active and balanced, the horse must move freely and rhythmically, responsive to the unspoken directions of the rider. It is not an easy undertaking with a high-couraged horse that is bursting with health and vigour, but the Master will contrive to put up an impressive, polished performance which rivets the attention and compels admiration.

Next day comes the speed and endurance test which, in a three-day event, is divided into four phases, the competitors setting off in turn at regular intervals. Phases A and C are roads and tracks, totalling between 10 and 20 km, with an easy time allowance; Phase B is a steeplechase course of roughly 3–4 km and three fences per kilometre, taken at the gallop, with steep time penalties; after a 10-minute break for a veterinary check on the horse's condition comes Phase D, a cross-country course of some 5–8 km, with an average of four obstacles—fixed and solid and of generally natural appearance—to the kilometre, to be completed at the gallop and carrying half the rate of time penalties for the steeplechase, but with

Major John Anderson became the B.H.S.'s second technical adviser in 1970 and is chiefly responsible for events in the south.

heavy penalties for refusals, circling or falling at the obstacles.

The Master will have his calculations of distance and timing carefully prepared—probably strapped to his wrist with his chronometer—and will settle his horse into a steady, rhythmic stride, taking all the obstacles smoothly and without hesitation. He will make it all look deceptively easy and he and his horse will arrive at the finish apparently fresh as a daisy.

On the final day the horses are trotted up for another veterinary inspection and then follows the show jumping test. This is not a particularly difficult test in itself but, seen in its context as the climax to three gruelling days of competition, when horses and riders are often tired, stiff and sore, it takes on a quite different significance from any other show jumping contest.

The Master will appear quite unruffled throughout, able to concentrate his own and his horse's efforts on jumping every fence with precision and accuracy, and putting out of his mind the thought of what may be at stake.

When all is said and done, it is the cross-country course designer who holds the key to the whole competition. Within the perfectly reasonable restrictions on speed, distance and size of obstacles laid down by the rules, he must set a course on his own piece of ground which will really stretch the competitors and produce a worthy winner, but without ravaging the less competent members of the field.

He must know exactly what a horse is capable of and what it is fair to expect. Some know this from personal experience, some by instinct, but even the best of them have a sleepless night before their course is jumped on the big day and not one can relax until the first clear round has proved that it really can be done.

Course design is a highly skilled job, fence construction a task for the craftsman, and there are few really expert practitioners about. It is also a very heavy responsibility and for this reason the Fédération Equestre Internationale appoints impartial technical delegates to inspect and approve the course

Major Noel Palmer joined the B.H.S. staff in 1972. The technical advisers not only design and build cross-country courses but are towers of strength to organisers on the day of competition, turning their hand to any task and dealing with any emergency.

at international events. Even so, they sometimes get it wrong.

The difficulty of a cross-country obstacle lies less in its sheer size than in its design and its siting in relation to the ground and to other obstacles. The more massive and solid the obstacle looks, the more inviting it will appear to the horse; whereas an "airy" fence, built of insubstantial materials, will seem hazardous. There are endless permutations of obstacles and almost as many more variations in the type of terrain, the rise and fall of the ground, the climate and weather conditions. All have their effect on the competition and all take their toll of competitors.

Long roads and tracks, ridden on a hot day in a humid climate, will obviously take much more out of horse and rider than the same distance in brisk, bracing conditions. This endurance factor has a great bearing on the difficulty of the subsequent cross-country course and must be taken into account by both course designer and competitor.

At the Mexico Olympics in 1968, speed and endurance day started fair and sunny, but later the heavens opened, the many streams turned into raging torrents which burst their banks and most of the course was a fearful, slippery mud-bath. The horses and riders who successfully completed it towards the end of the day became heroes overnight. But the technical delegate, knowing the quirks of the climate at that altitude and time of year, kept the dimensions of the obstacles well within bounds. The same sort of thing happened, less dramatically, at Montreal in 1976.

At Munich in 1972, the weather was hot and dry, the ground baked rock-hard and very dusty. The roads and tracks had to be long, in order to cover the distance between steeplechase and cross-country course sites, so Phase D was kept to a reasonable length, while the difficulty of the obstacles called for tactical rather than sheer jumping skill.

The riders study the course beforehand and so can plan their strategy. The horses have no such advantage. They must put their faith in their riders, confident that, if they are asked to tackle even a completely strange hazard, it must be all right; and they often perform prodigies of bravery in face of the unknown. The one unforgivable crime on the part of a course designer is to spring a trap on a horse, causing him an unfair surprise, because a brave and well-trained horse will attempt even the impossible if it is required of him by the rider in whom he trusts.

Horses, like humans, are very different and an experienced rider will adjust his entire approach to the cross-country accord-

ingly. This is just one more challenge to those, like Lorna Sutherland, Bill Roycroft and Mark Phillips, who have ridden three horses round Badminton, for instance: a total of some 50 miles' hard riding and close

Mark Phillips clearing the
90th obstacle of the day,
having ridden three horses.

on 150 obstacles surmounted in one day!

Over the years there have been some notorious fences at big international events—fence 29 at Punchestown World Championships in 1970, for example, fence 23 at Munich Olympic Games in 1972, fence 2 at Kiev European Championships in 1973—much criticized, respectively, for their flimsy materials, siting, awkward spacing. They caused many falls and a lot of penalties, yet they cannot be said to have been unjumpable. There were plenty of skillful riders on bold horses who not only tackled them with complete success but almost made them look easy.

Fence 2 at Kiev The first horse to try this fence was Iller, ridden by G. Bengsston of Sweden, who finished up with the horse straddling the leading pole.

Fence 2 at Kiev The second horse to go was Syelles, ridden by N. Serschen of Austria. Note the position of the back legs in the first picture.

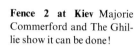

Fence 2 at Kiev Majorie Commerford and The Ghillie show it can be done!

Occasionally some quite new type of obstacle will appear, such as the Helsinki steps or the Normandy bank. They cause a great stir and much scratching of heads by competitors, but course designers are quick to snap up new ideas and try them out again. Soon such fences become household names and almost any horse will jump them with ease.

As the list of international events grows and the number of horses and riders in all interested countries increases, so the exchange of ideas quickens and the standard of course design rises.

If all that is to be learned from this book shows three-day eventing as an interesting and challenging sport to take part in, it makes it a fascinating one to watch. The

charm of setting out on foot across unspoiled country, the thrill at the sound of the steward's whistle which warns of a horse's approach, the excitement, spiced by the element of danger, as the competitor forms up to some awe-inspiring obstacle, the elation at a brilliant feat of jumping or superb piece of horsemanship, the agony of suspense when the fate of a national team is in the balance, are incomparable.

Most of the countries in which eventing flourishes draw big crowds to their well-established events, but it is a very expensive sport to organize and it needs every bit of financial support it can get.

Britain is extremely fortunate in having commercial sponsors, Whitbread's for Badminton, Raleigh for Burghley, and the Midland Bank (or their Scottish colleagues, the Clydesdale Bank) for virtually every other one-, two- or three-day event in the calendar. Without this most generous backing, it is hard to see how the sport could survive in its present sturdy form in this country.

Another very encouraging feature is the way so many successful and experienced riders, on retiring from active competition or even sooner, are taking up course-building or the organization of events. They have a tremendous contribution to make to what is still a genuinely amateur sport, bringing little in the way of material reward and heavily dependent upon the energy and enthusiasm of its own practitioners.

But there is still much to be done. As costs of every kind are steeply rising, so is the expense of forage, saddlery, transport and professional tuition. There are fewer and fewer people who can afford to buy and keep top-class horses, fewer still who have both the time and the talent to train and ride them.

A rider needs not one but a succession of horses in the pipeline and must be adding to his own experience all the time if he is to succeed. It is said to take four years to produce an international three-day event horse but, so taxing is the event itself, there are comparatively few opportunities to compete in the course of a year and even the top prizes can only make a contribution towards the overall expense involved.

But still the popularity of three-day eventing grows, with competitors, organizers and spectators alike, in more and more countries. This has repercussions in the spread of knowledge on the care and training of horses and the general standard of riding and so, indirectly, benefits the horse world as a whole. The horse world will surely find ways to strengthen and expand such a marvellous sport and to keep the Masters of eventing in the saddle.

A
Three-day
Event
Schedule

By kind permission of the British Horse Society, we have reproduced a section from the Omnibus Schedule for the 1977 Autumn Horse Trials which was distributed in June. The proper organisation and control of Combined Training is a vital part of the success of the sport and would-be competitors may be interested to see a little of what is involved.

BRITISH HORSE SOCIETY
WYLYE HORSE TRIALS
(International Three-Day Event C.C.I.)
at
Bathampton House, Wylye, Wiltshire.
on
Friday, Saturday, Sunday and Monday
23rd, 24th, 25th and 26th September, 1977

Hon. Organisers:	Lord & Lady Hugh Russell, Bathampton House, Wylye, Wiltshire.
Secretary:	Miss Fiona Lyndon-Skeggs, Bathampton House, Wylye, Wiltshire.
	(Tel: Wylye 281—Office hours ONLY please)
Technical Delegate:	C.C.I.—Major A. L. Rook, M.C.
	National Novice—Major W. J. Pinney

1. CLASSES
    Midland Bank Open: C.C.I. (International Three-Day Event) open to all grades.

    Midland Bank Novice:
    National Three-Day Event for Grade III horses only at 30th June, 1977.
    This class will probably be divided into two sections.

    Novice horses upgrading after 30th June will remain in the class for which they are entered.

2. QUALIFICATIONS for National Entries
    (a) Owners and riders must be members of the British Horse Society, and of the Combined Training Group.
    (b) Horses must be registered with the British Horse Society, and foaled in or before 1971.

    Midland Bank Open
    (c) Riders must be 18 years or over within the calendar year of the competition, and hold a current Amateur or Professional licence. At entry horses and riders must have completed at least two official horse trials, including one at Intermediate or higher level, or any Three-Day Event, including Junior Three-Day Event. Horses must have gained a minimum of 6 points in official competitions.
    All horses must hold an official F.E.I. Passport.

    Midland Bank Novice
    (d) Riders must be 17 years or over within the calendar year of the competition.
    At entry riders must have completed at least two official horse trials and horses must have gained at least three points.

    To start in both competitions horses and riders must have completed at least one official horse trial in 1977.

3. PROVISIONAL TIMETABLE (these times are subject to alteration)
    Thursday, 22nd September

1.00 pm	Briefing of competitors followed by a conducted tour of Phases A, B, and C.

    Friday, 23rd September

8.30 am	First Horse Inspection
11.30 am	Dressage: Midland Bank Novice
11.30 am	Dressage: Midland Bank Open

Saturday, 24th September
9.00 am	Speed and Endurance: Midland Bank Novice
9.00 am	Dressage: Midland Bank Open

Sunday, 25th September
10.30 am	Speed and Endurance: Midland Bank Open

Monday, 26th September
9.30 am	Final Horse Inspection
11.30 am	Jumping: Midland Bank Novice
1.30 pm	Prize Giving (mounted): Midland Bank Novice
2.00 pm	Jumping: Midland Bank Open
4.00 pm	Prize Giving (mounted): Midland Bank Open

4. PRIZES

The prize money for all sections has been generously donated by the Midland Bank Limited. 1st and 2nd prize winners in each Novice section will qualify for the 1978 Novice Championships; the first six in the Open class will qualify for the 1978 Midland Bank Open Championships.

Midland Bank Novice		Midland Bank Open	
1st	£60	1st	£300
2nd	£45	2nd	£200
3rd	£30	3rd	£120
4th	£25	4th	£80
5th	£20	5th	£60
6th	£15	6th	£40
7th	£10	7th	£30
8th	£10	8th	£30
9th	£10	9th	£30
10th	£10	10th	£30

Further prizes of £20 (Open Class) and £10 (Novice Classes) for every four additional starters over 40.

SPECIAL PRIZES

At the time of going to press it is not possible to list all the special prizes but they will include the two following; please state if you are eligible for these prizes on your entry form:

The Hunter Improvement Society Trophy for the best score by a horse sired by a H.I.S. premium stallion.

A saddle kindly presented by the Worshipful Company of Saddlers for the highest placed competitor under 21 in the Open Class.

5. ENTRIES

(a) All entries close at 9.00 am on Friday, 26th August and must be sent to the Horse Trials Secretary, Bathampton House, Wylye, Wiltshire. Please do not post entries before Monday, 18th July and envelopes should be clearly marked Horse Trials Entry. Cheques to be made payable to Wylye Horse Trials. A stamped addressed envelope would be appreciated.

(b) The entry fee for both classes will be £10 per horse of which £8 will be refunded to competitors who withdraw, in writing, before 9.00 am on 26th August. There will be no refund on horses withdrawn after the close of entries.

(c) Entry forms not showing complete qualifications of entry will be returned. Qualifications should state competitions completed by horse and rider with event, year and class, also total points gained by horse must be shown on the entry form.

(d) No rider may ride more than four horses, not more than two of which may be entered in one class. If two or three horses are to be ridden any preference for order of riding will have to abide by the order of draw. The draw will be made at the close of entries on 26th August and the starting order cannot be changed thereafter.

(e) Entries will be acknowledged immediately after the Ballot date (1st August) and probable dressage day given. If this day is difficult for the rider please notify the secretary immediately in writing (see previous paragraph re-starting order).

(f) Entries may have to be limited, in which case they will be dealt with as stated in Part 1 of the omnibus Schedule.

(g) Open class entries must state on their entry form the full name of their official groom (see paragraph 6a).

(h) Open class entry riders must hold a current Amateur or Professional licence and their horses should have an official F.E.I. passport.

Applications for both these should be made to the British Horse Society.

6. RULES

(a) Midland Bank Open will be run in accordance with F.E.I. Rules for Three-Day Events.

N.B. Competitors are reminded that under Article 311 of the above rules only the following personnel are allowed to ride or exercise an entered horse for the three days preceeding the event and for the entire duration of the competition.

The entered rider of the horse, another individual entered competitor of the same nation or the official groom to the said horse (see Entries paragraph 5(g)).

(b) Midland Bank Novice will be run as above except when modified as for Novice Three-Day Events under British Horse Society Combined Training Rules 1977.

7. DRESSAGE TESTS

Midland Bank Open: F.E.I. Three-Day Event Test 1975
Midland Bank Novice: British Horse Society Dressage Test No. 12
N.B. Spurs must be worn in both classes for the dressage phase.

8. SPEED AND ENDURANCE TESTS

Phase A—Roads and Tracks

Length approximately 4560 metres at a speed of 240 metres per minute.

Exceeding optimum time will incur one penalty point for each second up to the time limit which is one-fifth more than the optimum time.

Phase B—Steeplechase

Midland Bank Open:—Length 3450 metres at a speed of 690 metres per minute over 10 regulation British Steeplechase fences (including two open ditches).

Midland Bank Novice:—Length 1725 metres at a speed of 690 metres per minute over five regulation British Steeplechase fences (including one open ditch).

Competitors exceeding the optimum time in both classes will incur 0.8 of a penalty point for every commenced second up to the time limit.

Phase C—Roads and Tracks

Length approximately 9120 metres. Speed and penalties as for Phase A.

Phase D—Cross-Country

Midland Bank Open—Length between 5200 metres and 5700 metres at a speed of 570 metres per minute. There will be between 25 and 30 fences the maximum height of which will be 3′ 11″ (1.20 metres) with a maximum spread at the top of 5′ 11″ (1.80 metres) and a maximum spread at the base of 9′ 0″ (2.80 metres). However these maximum dimensions are unlikely to be used and the course will be designed in severity as for a Standard Three-Day Event to encourage the Intermediate level of horses.

Midland Bank Novice—Length between 4500 metres and 5000 metres with approximately 25 fences to be ridden at a speed of 520 metres per minute.

Dimensions of fence as for a Novice One-Day Horse trials.

In both classes competitors exceeding the optimum time will incur 0.4 of a penalty point for every commenced second up to the time limit.

9. JUMPING TEST

The course for both classes will be approximately 800 yards with 10 to 12 obstacles.

Midland Bank Open: Jumping test will be run under F.E.I. rules for Three-Day Events. N.B. A maximum height of 3′ 11″ (1.20 metres) to be ridden at a speed of 400 metres per minute (with five penalties for a knock down).

Midland Bank Novice: Jumping Test will be run under B.H.S. rules for Novice Three-Day Events. N.B. A maximum height of 3′ 9″ (1.5 metres) to be ridden at a speed of 300 metres per minute (with five penalties for a knock down).

10. WEIGHT

A minimum weight of eleven stone, eleven pounds (75 kg) will be carried in the Speed and Endurance and Jumping tests in BOTH CLASSES.

11. INSPECTION OF THE COURSE AND BRIEFING
Briefing of competitors followed by a conducted inspection of Phase A, B and C will be at 1.00 pm on Thursday, 22nd September.
Phase D (Cross Country) will be open for inspection from 10.00 am on Thursday, 22nd but the other phase will NOT be open until after the briefing.
Phase A and C may be inspected by vehicle but Phase B (Steeplechase) and D (Cross Country) may ONLY be inspected on foot.
It is regretted that transport cannot be provided for inspection of the roads and tracks where a Land Rover or similar type vehicle will be required.

12. WITHDRAWALS and DECLARATIONS
Withdrawals of all non-runners must be made by 9.00 pm on Tuesday, 20th September, either in writing or by telephone (Wylye 281) between 6 pm to 9 pm on Monday, 19th or Tuesday, 20th September. Please note these are the ONLY times and days when telephone withdrawals will be accepted.
Presentation of a horse, subsequently passed fit, at the first horse inspection will be taken to be the final declaration.
The organisers would be grateful if competitors, who have to withdraw after the close of entries, would notify them as soon as possible in writing. Non-presentation of a horse at the first horse inspection is not, in itself, sufficient withdrawal action.
Non-runners failing to withdraw according to the above conditions will be liable to be refused permission to compete in Horse Trials for a period of up to three months.

13. OBJECTIONS
Any objection during the competition must be made, in accordance with F.E.I. General Regulations, in writing personally to the President of the Ground Jury and be accompanied by a deposit of £5.

14. STARTING TIMES
Starting times will be available from the Secretary's tent each day and will be posted at Salisbury Racecourse stables. (These will also be available by telephone at Wylye 281 between 7 pm and 9 pm but please avoid telephoning if possible.)

15. HORSE INSPECTIONS
The horse inspections on Friday, 23rd September and Monday, 26th September will take place on the ground and both classes will be inspected simultaneously by different panels on each occasion.
The first horse inspection will be run in programme order.
The second horse inspection on Monday, 26th—the horses will be inspected in reverse order of merit following the speed and endurance day results. This order of inspection will be available to competitors on the previous evening. The show jumping phase will also take place in reverse order of merit.
Grooms MUST wear their horses' numbers for the horse inspections and horses brought forward without numbers and/or late, or not submitted, for either inspection will be eliminated from the competition.
Open Class only:—The Official F.E.I. passport for each horse MUST be produced at the First Horse Inspection.

16. MEMBERSHIP SCHEME
This year riders and owners of entered horses may become Wylye Horse Trials Members at a special rate of £6 (normal rate £8) provided their membership application is received before Wednesday, 14th September.
Membership privileges include a free Rover car pass enabling members to move their car about the ground to watch the dressage, show jumping and cross-country (the member's cross-country car parks give a view over three-quarters of the fences). The members' tent, which also overlooks the course, serves hot meals and has a licensed bar.
Competitors car passes will ONLY admit them to the Horse Box park and competitors car park at the cross-country box.
Competitors and owners wishing to enjoy the full advantages of the membership scheme should send in their application with their entry.

17. STABLING and ACCOMMODATION
    (a) Stabling and some grooms' accommodation will be available at Salisbury Racecourse, by the kind permission of the Racecourse committee. The Racecourse is nine miles from the event.
    (b) Stabling will cost £3 per horse per night if booked in writing before the close of entries (26th August). After the close of entries stabling may be booked at £4 per horse per night up to Friday, 16th September after which no stabling bookings will be taken.
    (c) Up to Friday, 16th September stabling cancellations will receive a refund (minus 50p per horse per night). After 16th September there will be no refund on any cancellations of stabling or grooms accommodation.
    (d) All loose boxes will be provided with straw bedding unless shavings are requested in writing on the stabling form. Hay and other foodstuffs can be provided if booked in advance.
    (e) The Racecourse has a limited amount of grooms' accommodation in two heated dormitories, one for men and one for women, equipped with bunks and some bedding. The charge will be £1 per person per night and all grooms' accommodation must be booked in writing and paid for, before Friday, 16th September. There will be no refund on cancellations after this date.
    (f) The Racecourse canteen will be open for breakfast and evening meals throughout the duration of the event.
    (g) Competitors must make their own accommodation arrangements. A list of nearby hotels can be sent if requested; please enclose a stamped addressed envelope.

18. CARAVANS
    (a) Caravans at the stables may be parked at a charge of 75p per night. Competitors wishing to bring their caravans MUST state this on their stabling form and send the appropriate money; they will then be sent parking cards for each night booked to allow them access to the Racecourse caravan park.
    (b) Caravans at Wylye Horse Trials may be parked on the ground in a site, with limited facilities, near the cross-country course and the charge will be £8 for the duration of the event (£4 for Wylye Members, see paragraph 15). Sites must be booked and paid for in advance.
    (c) It is recommended that anyone wishing to hire a caravan should contact Green Pennant Caravans Limited, London Road, Salisbury (telephone Salisbury 4979).

19. LOCATION
    The Wylye Three-Day Event is held at Bathampton House which is on the A36 Salisbury/Warminster road on the Salisbury side of the junctions with the A303 and NOT in Wylye village itself. Competitors coming on the A303 should leave Wylye By-Pass following the signs marked A36 Salisbury.
    Salisbury Racecourse Stables will be signed from the Horse Trial ground and off the A30 between Salisbury and Wilton.